Palette and Tomahawk
The Story of George Catlin

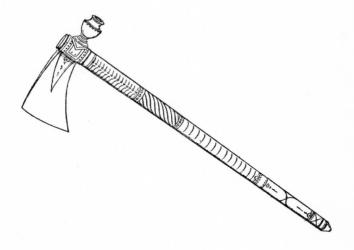

Palette and Tomahawk

The Story of George Catlin

July 27, 1796–December 23, 1872

by

Robert Plate

Illustrations from drawings
by GEORGE CATLIN

DAVID McKAY COMPANY, INC.,

New York

1962

PALETTE AND TOMAHAWK

COPYRIGHT © 1962 BY ROBERT PLATE

LIBRARY OF CONGRESS CATALOG CARD NUMBER 62–18967

MANUFACTURED IN THE UNITED STATES OF AMERICA

Pawnee Redstone Pipe

CONTENTS

ACKNOWLEDGMENTS

Grateful acknowledgment is made for the generous assistance received from: The New York Public Library; The New York Historical Society; The American Museum of Natural History, New York; The Woodstock Library of Woodstock, New York; and John C. Ewers, Assistant Director of the Museum of History and Technology of the Smithsonian Institution.

Special thanks are due to the New York Historical Society for permission to use the Catlin drawings and to the National Collection of Fine Arts of the Smithsonian Institution for the portrait of George Catlin by William H. Fisk.

Illustrations

Mandan Warrior

1: The Mark of the Indian

Now AND then a woodlark sang in that dark and lonely ravine. Occasionally the wind mourned through the hemlocks and firs. Mosquitoes whined; flies buzzed. But only one sound endured in the smothering hush of the deep woods: the murmur of the stream that coursed twenty feet below the rock ledge where the ten-year-old boy lay in wait.

The rifle beside George Catlin was too long for him, too heavy for him, and probably too dangerous for him. All this he knew, but he was too excited to care. His dark-blue eyes gleamed, intent on the salty spring that bubbled up near the creek. That salt lick lured all kinds of wild animals. Above all, it lured deer.

George had never fired a rifle. He had never killed a deer. Today he meant to do both.

I

In 1806 any boy growing up in Oc-qua-go, the wild Broome County valley of southern New York State, learned to fish and hunt almost as soon as he could walk. The deadly long rifle, however, had been forbidden to George by his father. George had needed only a small single-barreled shotgun to add a bounty of ducks, quail, pheasants, rabbits and squirrels to the dining table of the Catlin farm.

Now George patted the rifle confidently, picturing his trophy: a great buck with eyes glowing like lanterns, and a spread of antlers like the roots of an oak!

Once he brought home the venison surely his father would forgive his use of the rifle. Or—would he? Putnam Catlin was not easily swayed.

Before clearing a farm out of the wilderness, Mr. Catlin had been a lawyer in a brawling river town forty miles to the south, Wilkes-Barre, Pennsylvania. It was there that George had been born on July 27, 1796. As an infant still in his mother's arms George had made the rough trek to the farm. Tilling the soil, though, had not altered the cool legal mind of Putnam Catlin. A thoughtful man who loved to pore over thick books, he was not likely to be awed by any feats of his fifth child. He had forbidden the rifle—and that was that.

George sighed at the thought, but did not stir from his perch. He stretched out his hickory-tough little body, and waited. As the long afternoon hours slowly passed, shadows lengthened and the ravine darkened. George's limbs stiffened. His joints ached from the chill of the stone ledge.

And then—

A sound in the distance of crackling leaves! A sound of dainty, hesitant footsteps, coming closer and closer. George licked his dry lips; he wiped sweat from his palms; he clutched the rifle.

Moments later a deer stepped into the clearing beside the creek.

A buck! A giant buck! George thought.

The deer entered the pool and licked the salt. With the rifle cocked and firm on the rock, the shot would be easy.

Nothing required now, but a squeeze of the trigger. How simple! And how difficult it suddenly became, for the splendor and beauty of the tawny creature smote George with all the symptoms of buck fever. His teeth began to chatter. His body froze; he shivered and shook. His body burned with fever; sweat streamed down his brow. He tried to squeeze the trigger with paralyzed fingers that would not respond.

At the same time his mind whirled with dreadful ideas. Suppose the rifle was overloaded. It might explode; it might kill him! Even worse, much worse, suppose he shot—and missed!

While George tried desperately to master himself the deer lapped up its fill, stepped out of the pool, climbed the bank and disappeared into the brush. George almost wept.

"Oh, you fool!" he scolded himself. "You helpless little baby! He's gone—"

Just then the deer stepped back onto the bank, in clear view and even closer than before. It was a shot too easy to miss, and this time the boy's anger at himself

3

overcame the buck fever. Hot-eyed and tense but fully in control of himself, he sighted down the barrel at the unaware deer.

"Now!" he breathed silently. "My first buck!"

A rifle cracked. As if stung, the deer bounded a few yards. Then it collapsed on the bank, dead.

George gaped in stunned amazement. His own rifle was still unfired. The shot had come from a thicket to the left.

Too shocked to stir, with tears of frustration stinging his eyes, George bitterly awaited the appearance of the other hunter.

A tall form glided gracefully out of the forest toward the fallen deer. George gasped, and then clamped his jaws tight in sudden fear. For the hunter, drawing a large glittering knife from a sheath in the hollow of his back, was an Indian!

George tensely watched the copper-skinned hunter hang the deer by its hind legs from a tree limb to let it bleed. How horrifying to see his first real live Indian, and how fascinating! The Indian wiped his knife upon some moss, then relaxed on a tree trunk, drew a pipe from his pouch and lit it with flint and steel.

A thousand tales that George had grown up on suddenly became real.

Through this very valley Senecas and Cayugas with reddened tomahawks had retreated, along with Tories, after the fearful Wyoming Massacre of 1778. In that bloody battle at Wilkes-Barre George's Grandfather Sutton had swum across the Susquehanna under a storm of bullets and arrows to become one of the few male survi-

4

vors. George's mother, Polly Sutton, then only seven years old, had been captured by the Indians after the downfall of Forty Fort.

His mother had been unharmed after the capture, but what of the merciless slaughter beforehand? And now one of the red killers was only sixty feet away!

On one hand, George was fascinated by Indians. In fact he was building a little Indian museum of objects turned up by the plow in his father's fields. There were skulls, beads, flint arrowheads and even the head of an Indian pipe tomahawk.

On the other hand, George was terrified by Indians. The yarn-spinning travelers who often held forth at the Catlin fireside aimed at excitement, not truth. Inevitably the ferocity of the Indian was greatly magnified.

"What's an Injun?" one scarred old trapper and Indian fighter had demanded last night. "A scalper, a drunkard, a thief, a killer!"

"You must admit their courage," Putnam Catlin calmly retorted. "And their customs, if you trouble to look at them, are often admirable. They worship their God, they love and cherish their children—"

"Bah! A good Injun is a dead Injun!" And here the trapper yanked off his coonskin cap to expose a scarred and naked pate, on which only a thin rim of hair remained. "Left me for dead, the varmints did, and scalped me!"

In a quick murmur of assent most of those present agreed that Indians were a lower race and a nuisance—so many wolves to be wiped out.

"If you don't kill the Injun, he'll kill you. It's that

5

simple," pronounced the trapper, and then went on to spill gore in tales of massacres and tortures perpetrated by red fiends—in all of which the trapper proved himself a man of great daring who always outwitted the fiends at the last moment.

"If you don't kill the Injun, he'll kill you." The words ran through George's brain now. He noted how cool and steady his hand had become. With his rifle still loaded, he had nothing to fear. One bullet could end the menace.

Just because he was a small boy, was that any excuse to cower and run? After all, at the age of twelve Putnam Catlin had enlisted to serve with the Second Connecticut Regiment for six years throughout the Revolutionary War. As a fife-major participating in many actions against the British, he had set a brave example for his sons.

If he sees me, I'll be scalped, George thought. He shifted the rifle at the hunter. It's him or me!

As George sighted at the broad back of the dreadful enemy, the man turned. He puffed contentedly on his pipe, smoke curling blue ribbons from his mouth and nostrils. At peace with the world, the hunter cocked his head to appreciate the trill of a woodthrush. A faint smile of satisfaction played about his lips as he looked at the deer.

A strange feeling of kinship overwhelmed the watching boy. Why, this Indian was no fiend! He was just— just what? Why, just a *man,* that's all. An Indian, yes, but even more important, a man and a fellow human being.

6

George's hands slackened on the rifle. He calmly watched the Indian finish his smoke, tie the deer's fore and hind legs together, and sling the deer upon his back. Rifle in hand, the Indian disappeared down the old road that led toward the Catlin farm.

George leaped to his feet. To avoid the road the Indian had taken, he clambered up a steep cliff, then raced helter-skelter through the woods for home to spread the great news. The woods were already dark with approaching night. In his mad dash the boy lost the rifle.

His shouts were heard long before he reached the farmstead: "I've seen an Indian! I've seen an Indian!"

Charles and Henry, George's two oldest brothers, were away at school, but the younger Catlins made a willing audience. Clara and Juliette, aged fourteen and twelve, ran out from the kitchen to greet him, their hands still sticky from preparing bread dough. Eliza, eight, James, six, and Mary, four, jumped up and down with excitement as George gasped out his tale. Two-year-old Julius ignored him in favor of mud pies, however, and the infant Lynde squawled away in his crib.

Old Grandpa Sutton testily cut short George's glorious yarn with a sharp "Tush! No Indians been hereabouts in years."

A hired hand chimed in. "The lad's Injun collection has gone to his head," he said darkly. "That sprout dreams too much for his own good!"

George's lips trembled as the skeptical elders derided his story. Seeing his agitation, Putnam Catlin mildly told him to calm down and go to bed. Tomorrow would be soon enough to explain about the rifle.

A few minutes later, as George sobbed into his pillow, the bedroom door opened and his mother entered the room.

"Nobody believes me," he sobbed. "But I'm not lying."

"I believe you, dear," Mrs. Catlin said, and rested a hand gently on his quivering shoulders. "Of course you saw an Indian. Now go to sleep."

Early the next morning, acting on the report of a hired hand, Putnam Catlin took his chastened son to the far end of a wheatfield. George's eye widened at sight of a miniature encampment.

There, sizzling a venison steak over a fire, was the Indian hunter! Beside him sat his wife and ten-year-old daughter. A blanket suspended above them screened out the sun.

Putnam Catlin clapped his son on the shoulder. "You were right, son," he said. "Indians, sure enough."

Then Mr. Catlin courteously approached the Indian, saying "How-how-how," and the two men took each other by the hand.

The Indian, who spoke some English, explained that he was an Oneida from the Cayuga Lake country, more than a hundred miles distant. On-o-gong-way (A Great Warrior) then stuffed fresh tobacco in his pipe, lit it, and gravely passed it to Mr. Catlin for a few puffs and then to George, as a pledge of friendship.

While Mr. Catlin related the story of his son's frustrated hunt, George burst into a fit of coughing from the pipe smoke. The Indian waited for George to stop choking, and then took him by the hands, saying warmly,

8

"Good. Good hunter. Some of the venison is yours." Whereupon he presented George with a small saddle of the venison.

The smallness of the saddle surprised George. Yesterday his fevered eyes had pictured a huge buck, but it must have been a small deer indeed. The Indian had seemed gigantic, too. Now, in the cool light of morning, and in the comforting presence of Putnam Catlin, On-o-gong-way seemed of ordinary size.

George thanked the Indian. Wondering why On-o-gong-way had made such a long and dangerous journey through a land where hunters considered Indians as fitting a target as woodchucks or weasels, he asked, "Why are you here, sir?"

The Indian hesitated. He looked intently at the Catlins for a moment. Then, accepting them as friends, he told his story.

"My father was one of the warriors in the great battle of Wyoming Valley," he began. Amusement glinted in his eyes at George's evident shock. "Yes. I was a boy like you at the time. In the retreat I carried many heavy objects taken from the whites—who had taken our land first. The hardest to carry, and the most valuable, was a kettle of gold."

Putnam Catlin exclaimed in surprise. George's spine tingled. Gold!

"I remember well," On-o-gong-way said, pointing to a nearby ravine, "white soldiers came charging through there. On these fields, then covered with trees, we fought a great battle. Many died. We learned that still another army of whites was advancing from the north. To escape we were forced to leave our canoes, and to flee across the mountains. We could not carry the heavy things over the hills. I saw my parents bury the kettle of gold at the foot of a tall pine tree, near the bridge."

"And you've come back to get it!" George cried. "Imagine, a kettle of gold. How big?"

The Indian extended his arms in such a great circle that his fingertips could barely meet. "So big," he said. But he gestured hopelessly at the plowed fields. "Once there were trees, now all is grass. Where can I look to dig, when the pine tree is gone? These green fields, my father," he said to Mr. Catlin, "were once our hunting grounds. We were many and strong. Now we are but a few. We live a great way off, and we are your children." He glanced anxiously at his wife and daughter. "The gold kettle would have made us rich."

"We'll dig up the whole field!" George exclaimed.

"Hold on," said Putnam Catlin. He sent George running back to the farmhouse to fetch a small brass kettle that had been plowed up a few years before at the very spot indicated by On-o-gong-way. When George panted back with the tiny kettle tucked under his arm On-o-gong-way took it in his hand and stared at it unbelievingly.

He shook his head, as if in horror, as Mr. Catlin told where the kettle had been found, and that it was made of brass, which looked like gold but was somewhat harder—and of much less value.

The Indian hefted the kettle, tried his knife on it, hefted it again as if unable to accept the truth. At last he said sadly, "It seemed so big; now it seems so little.

But it must be the same kettle. I was quite small. To small boys small things often seem large." (On this point, George, recalling the deer that had seemed so huge, heartily agreed.) "Some things grow larger in the mind over the years," he added.

George felt a sudden pang of sympathy for On-o-gong-way. This simple hunter had risked his life and that of his family for a worthless kettle. How many bright dreams had suddenly collapsed? But he stood erect, smiling ironically at his bitter disappointment as he tossed the tiny kettle to his daughter.

Putnam Catlin must have felt the same sympathy for the Indian's manly acceptance of misfortune.

"You are welcome to stay here," he said. "Stay as long as you like."

On-o-gong-way nodded gravely.

That day started a magic few weeks for George. With the aid of On-o-gong-way's keen eyes he soon found the lost rifle. And, once he had paid the penalty for its use by chopping a cord of firewood, he was free to spend all his time at the Indian bivouac.

He plagued On-o-gong-way with a torrent of questions on Indian lore, and always received full and fascinating replies. He brought the rusty tomahawk-pipe head from his collection, and On-o-gong-way carved a curiously decorated handle for it, perforated to permit smoking. Once the grindstone had burnished the blade bright and keen again, On-o-gong-way demonstrated the art of tomahawk throwing. From distances of ten or fifteen yards the Indian never failed to sink the whirling blade point first into the target tree. Soon the neighborhood boys were busily practicing this feat.

In later years George Catlin, ever 110 per cent on the side of the Indian, wrote: "The tomahawk (like the scalping knife, which generally has the Sheffield mark upon it) is a contrivance of civilized invention and construction, too deadly and destructive to have been made by the poor Indian."

Nevertheless, no matter how often they practiced, the boys never attained On-o-gong-way's deadly skill.

The simple, honest Indian family made many friends, and were always especially kind to George. On-o-gong-way shafted and feathered some of George's flint arrowheads, and ornamented them with woodpecker feathers. To hold the arrows the Indian made a fine quiver of fawnskin.

"George spends more time with the Indians than with us," Mrs. Catlin said one day to her husband.

He nodded. "They're fine people," he said, "but I'm worried about them. One day they'll want to return to their own people and they don't know how dangerous it will be. Somehow the rumor has spread that they actually have a big kettle of gold! News like that travels fast—especially among the forest brigands between here and Cayuga."

"Oh, dear!" exclaimed Mrs. Catlin. "The poor souls would never get through alive!"

"It will take a bit of money to send them home by a safe route," Catlin said, "but we'll scrape it up somehow."

The very next morning, however, the Indians disappeared as quietly as they had come. George found a farewell gift hanging in the woodhouse, a fine saddle of venison, decorated with an eagle quill from the headdress of On-o-gong-way.

For days thereafter George moped through his chores. Milking cows, chopping wood, feeding chickens—how artificial and dull it all seemed compared to the way of the Indian! But his brothers and sisters took to warwhooping and brandishing imaginary tomahawks at him every time they saw him, and soon their teasing restored his natural good humor.

Then occurred two fateful incidents.

One day, as George and two other ten-year-old boys practiced hurling his tomahawk, George carelessly stood too close to the tree as one of the other boys threw. The tomahawk glanced off the tree, felling George as the blade struck his left cheek and cut deep into the cheekbone.

The bloody accident left George with a wound several months in the healing. For the rest of his days he bore a long scar on his left cheek, the mark of the tomahawk—the mark of the Indian.

Far worse was the news that came some days later. In a valley ten miles away the body of On-o-gong-way was found, with two bullets in him. Nobody ever heard what became of his wife and daughter, or the pathetic "kettle of gold."

This tragedy, too, left an enduring scar on George Catlin. For the rest of his days he seethed with indignation at the injustice and cruelty visited upon Indians. To him, all Indians were friendly and noble and dignified

13

like On-o-gong-way. He raged as he saw how, in the long run, tribe after tribe of Indians got the same treatment as On-o-gong-way.

He continued to hunt and fish and play like any other boy, but once in a while, when he was alone at the old sawmill waiting for a trout to rise from the deep green pool, he would finger the scar on his cheek. The cheekbone ached. His heart ached, too, as he recalled On-o-gong-way.

Only ten, but the mark of the Indian was on George Catlin.

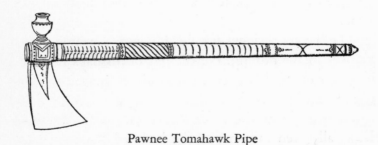

Pawnee Tomahawk Pipe

The Black Rock, a Sioux War Chief

2: Search for a Career

"WHAT AM I going to do with my life? What am I going to *be?*"

The great problem that concerns all youths troubled fifteen-year-old George Catlin as he leaned with his classmates against the white clapboards of the Wilkes-Barre Academy, enjoying a brief recess in the warm spring sunshine.

"Fine day for fishing, George," one of his friends teased. Everyone knew of George's love for rod and gun.

George sighed. The high water of the Susquehanna River sparkled temptingly. The pure streams hereabout abounded with trout, yellow perch, pike, catfish, bass, roach, shad—on and on, and George had caught them all.

Beyond the river the greening forests beckoned. That was his other home, rich with the fruits of wild plum, grape, butternut, crab apples, gooseberries; he knew them all, just as he knew the trees—ash, myrtle, and rock maple, pines, elm and beech, and giant buttonwoods, one twenty-one feet in girth.

An eager and expert student of the wilderness, George was already a master of woodcraft. Equally skillful with rifle and canoe paddle, he could always survive and flourish in the woods. However, he had to live in civilization, not the forest; therefore he must decide on a career.

At the moment, though, Wilkes-Barre did not appear particularly civilized. Two drunken men, pummeling each other, were rolling over and over in the sea of mud that was called a main street. As George looked away from the brawl, so common in this raw young river town, he heard a series of strange, far-off wails. His classmates stirred in excitement at the approaching sounds.

"A fleet of arks!"

The boys craned their necks to see the ungainly craft drifting into view. These shallow boxlike freighters bore grain and lumber all the way down the river to Chesapeake Bay. From the deck of each ark a crewman blew into a conch shell, which served as a boat horn. Other men guided the awkward freighters from the sternpost with pine sweeps thirty feet long.

The blare of horns grew almost unbearably loud. Small boys shouted and waved from the shore. The crewmen shouted and waved back. George waved, too, wishing he were a riverman drifting down the Susquehanna through counties he had never seen, on to the open sea and the world beyond. Next to hunting, fishing, and living like an Indian, George thought he'd like to travel.

But Putnam Catlin had other ideas.

"George," he had said, "with your retentive mind you should make a good lawyer."

Perhaps. But how much time do lawyers have to fish? How often do they travel? What contact do they make with Indians?

The arks drifted by, but George continued to stare at the sparkling river. His friends grinned knowingly. "Can't you just *see* the fish biting, George?"

The dreamer's quick smile flashed. "Yes. And if we don't get back inside soon Mr. Mallery will be biting, too!"

In spite of George's yen for the outdoors, he got along well with the headmaster. Garrick Mallery sensed the quality of this youth who combined the intense imagination of a dreamer with the high-spirited energy of a doer. In turn, George respected Mr. Mallery, who kept his students hopping with a study program of English, Greek and the classics, as well as history, geography, astronomy and mathematics. The tuition fee was five or six dollars a quarter.

The fading cry of the conch shells echoed faintly, sadly, as a forever-lost opportunity.

George braced his shoulders, turned his back on the lovely spring day, and dutifully filed back into the classroom. He was well aware of the sacrifices made to send him to school.

17

In 1807 Sally Catlin had been born. That made eleven children to feed. George, aged eleven, developed blisters learning how to steer a plow straight.

In 1809 Richard Catlin had been born. No blisters now for George, aged thirteen. Thick callouses protected his palms. His wiry body could labor all day in the fields —though he always found time to hunt or fish, or play "Indian" with his brothers.

And just a month ago, in March, 1812, John Catlin had been born. Now Putnam Catlin had to scrape a living for thirteen children out of the soil of his present farm at Hop Bottom, Pennsylvania.

Most parents would have kept a lively fifteen-year-old like George at the plow full time. Putnam Catlin, however, was more interested in cultivating minds than fields. He wanted his brood to be as well read as he in the classics, sciences, and arts. George's mind, he knew, was too bright to be wasted—so off he must go to school, no matter what the cost.

Most evenings at Hop Bottom Mr. Catlin read from good books to his family. There were evening prayers, too, by the flickering candlelight, for George's mother was a devout Methodist.

George had no intention of failing such parents. Nevertheless, the question of his destiny nagged him even in the classroom.

Lawyers, of course, were highly respectable. Unfortunately, the rousing tales of travelers who had been down the broad Ohio and across the mighty Mississippi to the mysterious lands and unknown tribes of Indians, only partly described by the great Lewis and Clark expedition of a few years before, made courtroom life seem dull and dusty-dry.

Only one aspect of the yarns repelled George: the typical callousness toward the redman. Listening to one-sided accounts of Indian battles and treacheries, George would finger the scar on his cheek and recall the murder of his good and gentle friend On-o-gong-way.

A lawyer he would be, if he must. A western explorer he would be, if he could. But he would never be an Indian hater or an Indian killer. Never!

"Mr. Catlin." A sharp Yankee voice broke into George's musings. "I trust we are not disturbing your dreams."

"No, sir!" George leaped to his feet, as his classmates tittered. "Not at all, sir! What is the question, Mr. Mallery, please?"

The headmaster surveyed the slight thin youth with the dark hair. The main trouble with this gifted student, he felt, was a lack of purpose. Most youths had the same lack, but were willing enough to drift passively through life, taking what came. Young Catlin was different. Intense, eager, he obviously yearned to hurl himself wholeheartedly into some thrilling endeavor. But who, in this mundane life, could realistically hope to find such a career? The poor lad was almost inevitably doomed to disappointment and boredom as a small-town lawyer.

It was all so youthful, so touching.

"No question," said Garrick Mallery gently. "Just pay attention, Mr. Catlin. The fish you cannot catch today, you can seek another time."

The big fish that George Catlin sought—a truly fitting career—seemed no closer as the busy years passed. He studied at school; he worked on the farm; he hunted and fished, especially with his younger brother Julius. He reached his full height, a bare five feet eight inches, and his full weight—a slight but tough and sinewy 135 pounds. Although troubled by poor hearing in one ear, from unknown causes, he was a light-hearted, good-looking youth, with dark hair and piercing blue eyes. Pretty girls began to eye him just as often as he eyed them.

In 1815 Francis, the last and fourteenth Catlin child, was born. George dandled the infant on his knee, predicted a great future for him—and privately wondered about his own future. He felt as aimless as a feather blown by the wind. With all the intensity of his nature he yearned to direct himself toward some great goal—but what?

Shortly before his twenty-first birthday, in 1817, Putnam Catlin happily announced that through careful saving the Catlins could send George to the eminent law school of Reeve and Gould in Litchfield, Connecticut, Mr. Catlin's birthplace.

"You're ready, George," his father said. "Mr. Mallery has done well. You write clearly. You know enough history and logic to hold your own with graduates of Princeton and Yale. You're at home in the classics." He hesitated, peering fondly at his son. "But you don't seem enthusiastic about a legal career."

George thought of his mother toiling over spindle and loom, of his father hunting for weary hours over account books for elusive pennies. "It's a wonderful opportunity," he said dutifully.

"Is there some other profession, perhaps, that you secretly have in mind—"

George shook his head. If only there were!

"Well then, good luck—and God bless you."

A dashing red coach, drawn by a four-horse team, pulled up to a halt. Young Mr. Catlin hopped out, clutching his few belongings.

A crack of the whip, a blare of the horn and the coach raced on, Boston-bound, leaving George coated with dust, and somewhat open-mouthed at his first view of Litchfield.

The elegance of the old town contrasted sharply with the raw newness of Wilkes-Barre. A quick leg-stretching exploration delighted George with the graciousness of the broad elm-arched streets and the handsome houses, impressed him with the prosperity of the busy shops, mills and factories.

Shyly, he called on relatives, Dr. Abel Catlin and old Grove Catlin, who ran the tavern on the Litchfield Green. The friendly welcome, especially from his cousins, Flora Catlin and Mary Peck, rather overwhelmed him.

"A handsome young man like you will have a grand time with the pretty girls at Miss Pierce's," they assured him. They both taught drawing at the Female Academy of Miss Sarah Pierce, on North Street. "Amateur theatricals, boating, sleigh-riding, sketching, picnics, parties!"

"And all of it chaperoned," Dr. Catlin said drily. "Very strictly chaperoned."

George blushed. As soon as he could, he excused himself and paid a visit to the law school.

Its appearance was disappointing. Situated directly behind Judge Tapping Reeve's large, impressive house on South Street, the school was a small, unheated building severely furnished with rock-hard benches.

The lessons of Reeve and Gould, he soon discovered, were just as hard as the benches. They were also very effective. In a span of some fifty years this small school produced several vice presidents, half a dozen cabinet members, many supreme court judges, senators, congressmen and governors, and hundreds of outstanding lawyers.

It was a fine place—if you wanted to be a lawyer.

In winter the only warmth came from the body heat of a hundred shivering students and the hot bricks tucked under their feet. George fumbled with numb fingers through layer after layer of clothing for his notebooks. Since he was hard of hearing in one ear, and Judge Reeve was physically incapable of speaking louder than a whisper, he was constantly straining to hear the lectures. Autumn, winter, spring, whatever the lure of the outdoors, George was there with the big impressive whispering man, whose long gray hair hung to his shoulders.

Oddly enough, the lessons he learned from the Female Academy were of far more consequence to his future. His teacher cousins taught him the use of crayon and brush. Fascinated, George soon was deftly turning out watercolor sketches that far surpassed those of his teachers.

Urged on by his cousins, he began to see more of the girl students. Poise replaced shyness as he became at home in the mansions of Litchfield, asparkle in the evenings with crystal and candlelight, gay with flowered crinolines for girls and pink-gingham frock coats for men.

One evening, directly after paying his respects to his wealthy host, George hurried to a room where some large portraits hung. First he squinted at the portraits from a distance for the overall effect; then he moved in close, searching out the details of brushwork and perspective with a concentration that far surpassed any he could give his textbooks.

"Mr. Catlin!" A soft hand tapped his shoulder; a pair of pretty blue eyes stared into his. "You're at a party—remember? Not a museum."

George straightened up with his ready smile, and gallantly offered his arm to the girl. "Now that you're here, pictures are driven clear out of my mind!"

Laughing, they joined the group in the drawing room, but the excitement of the paintings lingered with George. Before the evening ended art came up again, as guests passed about their miniatures.

Big portraits were fine for the rich and settled, but America was on the move. The only convenient picture for a traveler must fit into pocket or locket, thus the vogue for tiny portraits painted on ivory.

George studied the miniatures carefully. All present agreed that the very best were those painted by Anson Dickinson, a native of Litchfield.

"Beautiful work," George said. "Mr. Dickinson must have studied for years in Europe to attain such skill."

"Not at all. He's completely self taught."

"Really?" George looked even closer at the delicate painting. The likeness was perfect, the color fresh and

23

true. The work was vastly superior to his own crude sketches—but Dickinson had taught himself! Why couldn't he do the same? He thrilled to the hope of creating such beauty.

The new interest lightened the tedium of legal textbooks. As the months spun by, George sketched, drew and painted at every opportunity. Soon he did a portrait of Judge Tapping Reeve himself. Its execution gave him as much satisfaction as the certificate that the Judge handed to him on October 1, 1818, attesting that George Catlin had read law in their office and regularly attended the daily lectures.

Once his finals and bar examinations were successfully passed, George became a full-fledged lawyer. He bade farewell to Litchfield, and set up practice in Lucerne County, Pennsylvania.

Eventually Putnam Catlin turned up to see his lawyer son in action. Watching George in his office and in court, he saw that no matter how idle his son might be from lack of clients, he always kept busy. His pencil or charcoal moved incessantly, sketching everybody in view.

Mr. Catlin leafed through a series of sketches on brown paper, done with charcoal and white chalk. Then he looked at his son in astonishment.

"What on earth are *these* all about, George?"

The son grinned sheepishly. "I'm trying to catch impressions of character," he explained. "At night I sketch before the mirror. This one, for instance"—he held up a sketch of himself grimacing ferociously—"that's supposed to be rage. And here's joy, wonder, scorn, jealousy, ecstasy, and so on."

24

"You mean to say you spend your nights making faces at yourself in the mirror?" The farmer-philospher struggled hard to accept the idea of his brilliant son behaving in such absurd fashion.

"Only in a sensible cause, father," George said.

Mr. Catlin sighed. "They're good sketches—very good, in fact—but do you think it's entirely proper to sketch in the courtroom, too?"

"Oh, I'm not a bad lawyer," George said. "Did you hear about my defending the Irishman the other day? He had confessed—actually confessed—to stealing a broadaxe, and I convinced the jury they should clear him!"

"Ah!" The father beamed approval. "I knew your eloquence could work wonders, if ever you put your heart into it. Think of the good you can do. This Irishman must have been overcome with gratitude."

The lawyer burst into merry laughter. "Oh no! He was furious with me and the jury. He didn't mind being called a thief—but he couldn't stand to be called a liar!"

Shortly after Putnam Catlin left, shaking his head, George slipped a sketchpad into his pocket, took out his flyrod, locked his office and happily trudged off to the banks of the Susquehanna.

Years later Catlin wrote of this period as a lawyer: "During this time, fortunately or unfortunately, another and stronger passion was getting the advantage of me, that of painting, to which all my pleading soon gave way; and after having covered nearly every inch of the lawyer's table (and even encroached upon the judge's bench) with penknife, pen and ink, and pencil sketches of judges, jurors and culprits, I very deliberately resolved to convert my law library into paint pots and brushes, and to pursue painting as my future and apparently more agreeable profession."

The bold decision made, Catlin moved speedily. With the proceeds from the sale of the law library he set up a tiny studio on Walnut Street in Philadelphia, with a shingle hung outside:

GEORGE CATLIN, MINIATURE PAINTER

Without formal training, and with very little money, the young artist optimistically awaited trade. He had found his career at last, or it had found him.

Night and day he worked zestfully to perfect his skills. Only when he paused now and then to clear his head with a hike along the riverfront did a strange unease attack him. Something vital was still missing from the grand design of his life. Something wonderful, important, exciting—but what?

He shook his head, stared into the dark waters, then shrugged.

Whatever it was, he felt, he would surely find it— or it, too, would find him. Meanwhile, mustn't keep the world waiting. Back to the paints and brushes!

And he strode eagerly toward the studio.

Clermont, Head Chief of Osages

3: Search for a Cause

A SCREAMING WINTER wind stampeded clouds across the Philadephia sky. George Catlin, shoulders hunched under a threadbare jacket, plodded through the snowy streets without a thought for the stinging cold. The excitement of hope provided all the heat he needed.

Though March had just roared in, he dreamed of sunny May, month of the famous annual exhibition of the Pennsylvania Academy of Art, goal of painters young and old. He had already submitted a group of his latest miniatures to the exhibition committee.

His father had cautioned him not to expect too much. Putnam Catlin, bearing well the disappointment of his son's switch in professions, took a keen interest in the new career. "You're only twenty-four and untrained. Professionals with years of experience are often rejected

27

by the Academy. Don't let your optimism run wild."

George agreed. He must be practical, not a futile dreamer. And yet—his miniatures *were* good, weren't they? Of course! The committee didn't care whether you were twenty or eighty, trained or untrained, all they wanted was good work. So—!

Heady with dreams of glory, George entered Peale's fantastic Philadephia Museum.

His frequent visits to the museum never failed to stimulate, or perhaps overstimulate, him. After a few hours with its wonders he often felt pent up, and vaguely uneasy. Being an artist was fine, but was it enough?

Standing before the exhibits of the latest inventions, for instance—models of steam engines, sewing machines, new looms—he responded as if to a challenge. Somewhere within him must be the ingenuity to invent similar marvelous machines!

With his mind aboil over the potential of some new gadget, he would walk on to the unsurpassable collection of reptiles, birds, and animals, all handsomely mounted and arranged according to the classical order of Linnaeus by Charles Willson Peale and his talented family. A hundred years ahead of his time, Peale had so cleverly simulated the natural surroundings of his specimens that George would itch for rod, gun and a forest path.

The displays of insects and minerals would divert him to scientific thoughts of entomology and geology. And the huge mastodon skeleton, the first one ever assembled, dug up by the remarkable Mr. Peale himself—well!

Row upon row of portraits of the Founding Fathers might snap George back to his own career. But—look here at the Indian craftwork, part of the collection of the famous Lewis and Clark expedition. Listen to the live eagle scream from the rafters!

Today, though, even these marvels could not make him forget that his fate was being decided. Without official approval of one or two of his miniatures he could not hope to get enough orders to survive as an artist.

Still, Peale's Museum was always so lively and full of fun that his spirits lifted as soon as he stepped inside.

Charles Willson Peale, bent on having a family of artists, had given his sons names such as Rembrandt, Titian, Raphaelle and Rubens. Surprisingly, they were all excellent artists. Like the numerous other Peales, they did their bit for the museum. Mrs. Peale took tickets. One of the daughters thundered out a lively tune on the big organ. Rembrandt was lecturing to a large group gathered before the portraits of Indian chiefs of the eastern forests, not far from the life-size waxwork figures of the different races of the world. Seeing George, he gestured for him to wait.

George nodded in surprise. He barely knew Rembrandt; in fact he knew few of the well-established artists of Philadelphia, such as the Peales, Thomas Sully, and John Neagle. Although he made friends quickly, they were famous and accomplished men; he was only an unknown novice.

As he waited curiously for Rembrandt, he mused on the crowds thronging the museum halls. Why did these people, most of them with little love or knowledge of art and science, flock into Peale's? Shrewd old Charles Peale, George decided, knew human nature. To pull in the crowds you needed oddities, showmanship, excitement.

That accounted for the trigger finger of an executed murderer, the white blackbird, the gizzard of a Muscovy duck that had swallowed too many pins, and the dinner parties Charles Peale occasionally gave inside the skeleton of the huge mastodon. It accounted for the animated mechanical devices with music and elaborate sound effects, depicting the pageantry of Satan's palace as described by Milton, or showing the *Bonhomme Richard* bearing down with booming cannon on the *Serapis,* complete with wooden waves moving in the foreground, transparent clouds of curtains over the scene, and holes breaking open in the sails.

As he mused, he learned lessons that would affect his entire life.

Once Rembrandt Peale had finished his talk, he advanced toward George with a friendly smile. "Congratulations," he said heartily, extending his hand. George took it, wondering, hoping. Rembrandt was a member of the Academy. Could this mean—?

He moistened his dry lips. "Has one of my miniatures been accepted?"

Rembrandt shook his head. George tried hard to hide his disappointment. "Not one. Four. They'll be in the May exhibit."

Four! Four miniatures in the big show! George stammered his thanks as Rembrandt assured him that his works showed great promise. In a happy daze, he started to leave.

"Oh, one thing more," Rembrandt called after him.

"Please drop in at my studio. Sully and some of the others would like to meet you."

George practically flew back to the icy little studio on Walnut Street. This was his first triumph, and it tasted sweeter than honey.

In that year of 1821, when the Academy showed four of his miniatures, George Catlin won a local reputation and a growing number of commissions. He worked hard, he made moderate sums of money, he made many friends. He took time off to visit his brother Julius, now a cadet at West Point, and jubilantly relate his triumphs.

But through it all he suffered a strange undercurrent of discontent. Sometimes he chided himself. He had wanted to be a professional artist, and here he was, a professional artist by his twenty-fifth birthday. What was lacking? Why couldn't he relax and enjoy his modest successes?

A long and thoughtful letter from his father gave him something else to think about. Most eminent painters had worked at portraits and history, wrote Putnam Catlin. It would be wise for George to study such great masters, particularly those of the fifteenth and sixteenth centuries. In his clear but tiny hand, Mr. Catlin listed Renaissance artists as described in Vasari's *Lives*—da Vinci, Titian, Raphael, Michelangelo.

Touched by the detailed advice from his busy father, Catlin studied art history and kept busy with his painting. In 1822 the Academy exhibited six of his small portraits on ivory.

"You're on the way up!" exclaimed Cadet Julius Catlin.

On the way up indeed. In February of 1824 George received the coveted honor of election to the Pennsylvania Academy of Art as an Academician. A brief three years of intense study and labor had overcome his false start as a lawyer. At twenty-seven, he was hailed by his peers as one of the more accomplished painters of the day.

It was not enough.

His parents and family were proud of him; his colleagues liked and respected him. Within a few years his growing trade in miniatures would surely earn him a fine income.

But did he truly want to spend his life in cities, in the drawing rooms of the elite and wealthy?

The prospect seemed trivial. As Headmaster Mallery had sensed long ago, George craved some grand project into which he could throw himself heart and soul. In Catlin's words: "My mind was continually reaching for some branch or enterprise of the arts, on which to devote a whole lifetime of enthusiasm."

In his twenties, he still had a life to spend. He must spend it in some wonderful and exciting way, not on minuets and perfumed parties.

He was a man in search of a cause.

This need came partly from his desire to impress a logical design on his life. It came mainly from his awareness of a fuel within him that would burn brightly and passionately for a whole lifetime, if only he learned how to light it.

One day in the winter of his election to the Academy,

he visited his old haunt, Peale's Museum. A strange ⟨
egation of tall bronzed men, Indian chiefs from the
Western plains on their way back from Washington, w
being shown the exhibition.

George's heart leaped in sudden excitement at the
sight of them. He sidled closer to the chiefs, his painter's
eye sharp and appraising. The colorful outfits of skins,
war-eagle plumes, and pictured robes enthralled him.
The men were noble and dignified.

Immediately aware that destiny had assigned him a
mission, Catlin trailed them for hours, in a state of feverish joy. Before they left, the artist had reached these con-
clusions:

The drab clothing and drab civilization of the white
man spoiled all the beauty of Nature.

The best model for any painter was Man—but only
Man in a state of simplicity and unspoiled Nature. Therefore the country from which such men come—that is,
the Far West—must be the best studio and the best school
of art in the world.

But this best of all studios in a few short years would
be destroyed by the onrush of the corrupting white man.

"The history and customs of such a people, preserved
by pictorial illustrations, are themes worthy the lifetime
of one man," Catlin wrote later, "and nothing short of
the loss of my life shall prevent me from visiting their
country, and becoming their historian."

His flame was lit, never to die. He had found his
cause. He had yet to discover the many obstacles to the
fulfilment of that cause.

Red Jacket

4: Obstacles to the Cause

"I DON'T UNDERSTAND it, Cat," said Rembrandt Peale. He frowned in puzzlement at the Catlin brothers, George and Julius, who were visiting his studio.

George smiled faintly. Aware of his poor hearing, Rembrandt raised his voice. "Last year you had six miniatures in the Academy show, but this year you submitted only one. Why? You're just hitting your stride, Cat. Your reputation will grow, if you keep at it. Money will roll in—"

"Good!" exclaimed Julius cheerfully. A lively, adventurous youth eight years younger than George, he shared many of George's traits, including a talent for nature study and the arts. "It'll take lots of money to do what we want to do."

George admitted that he was painting so few miniatures now that he earned only a few dollars a week, for the barest of livings.

Rembrandt made a bewildered gesture. "You're kicking away a golden opportunity. And for what?"

"To prepare myself," George said simply. "To remove an obstacle."

Quickly, he outlined his determination to paint the Indians of the Far West. For this task the slow meticulous technique of miniature painting would be useless. He would have to work fast, under all sorts of uncomfortable and hazardous conditions. He must learn to catch character with a few quick slashes of the brush, and make the portraits life-size in the bargain. For months he had been studying every oil painting in Philadelphia, and practicing his effects so constantly that no time was left for making a living.

Julius interjected an excited recital of the wonders to come: a traveling museum of Indians, with hundreds of paintings of various tribes (George's job) and a vast collection of whatever affected the Indian way of life: animal, mineral, craftwork (Julius's job). It would be a sort of Peale Museum, but concentrating solely on the Indians of the Far West.

A noble project, Rembrandt observed respectfully. Then, noting George Catlin's thin, almost gaunt figure, he invited the young men to dinner.

Julius whooped. He was tired of eating like a mouse with his brother while on leave from West Point. "And we'll bring George's first crack at painting on canvas. Wait till you see it!"

The dinner was a great success, and so was the painting. A bold and expertly painted self-portrait (now hanging in the Thomas Gilcrease Institute), it shows Catlin as a handsome young man of twenty-seven, with strong features and luxuriant hair—as romantic as any portrait of the great romantic figure of that day, Lord Byron himself.

Peale and his influential colleagues were impressed. More important to George, it proved he had overcome an obstacle by developing a technique suitable for his cause. But many obstacles remained, some obvious—such as money—and others less so.

Money came first, for he was very poor, and well aware of the expense ahead for travel, equipment and funds to keep him alive for the many months in which he would not earn a penny.

Soon after George tackled the money problem, he had a piece of good fortune. He met William Leete Stone.

Stone, only four years older than Catlin, had much in common with him. He, too, had grown up in the frontier atmosphere of the upper Susquehanna, in New York State, and had also received a simple but sound classical training in Latin and Greek. Like George, he brimmed over with energy and determinaton.

At the age of sixteen Stone walked forty miles in a single night to offer himself as an apprentice to the editor of the *Cooperstown Federalist*. From that humble post he rose rapidly. Before he was thirty he reached the top of his profession, as a proprietor of the lively *New York Commercial Advertiser*. A strong-minded crusader, he fought for the emancipation of slaves, and the construction of the Erie Canal—a pet project of Governor DeWitt Clinton.

Best of all, William Stone collected Indian lore, great piles of manuscripts and books for a projected history of the Iroquois and the biographies he ultimately wrote of Red Jacket and Thayendanegea.

Immediately warming to George's ambitions, Stone forcefully assured the artist that fat public commissions would be forthcoming, and rich potential clients, too. Suddenly, he cracked his hands together. "Here's one, right under my nose! I'm publicity agent for the grand opening of the Erie Canal next year. We'll need lots of art work for that."

George nodded eagerly, captivated by the quick action of his dynamic new friend, who paced back and forth throwing out suggestions like firecrackers. "First you'll meet the governor," Stone said. "Yes, that's it. If he'll sit for a portrait or two your job will be that much easier. Nothing like a bit of prestige to put your work in demand."

"I can't thank you enough—" George began, but Stone cut him short by tugging him toward a corner of his office.

"Look here," he said. "Look at the material I've got on Red Jacket, the great Seneca orator. You must paint him sometime . . ."

Grateful to Stone for his newspaper's support, DeWitt Clinton readily received the young Pennsylvania artist, whose enthusiasms charmed him. The governor was delighted with this romantic but determined fellow who shared his scientific zeal for geology and the classification of American fish and birds.

December, 1824, found George Catlin in Albany, New York, painting his first portrait of Clinton, a miniature on ivory. For the next three years he was to benefit from the governor's influence. Clinton's introductions brought many portrait commissions in Albany and in the rapidly growing towns along the Big Ditch.

George was beginning the restless motion that filled much of his life. Business took him back and forth to New York, Litchfield, Hartford and to many small towns along the Erie Canal, and he often visited West Point to confer with Julius about their great Western dream.

He was on hand to see Julius graduate as a second lieutenant. The new officer greeted him jubilantly.

"Guess what?" Julius tossed a mock salute at his brother. "I'm assigned to the First U. S. Infantry— stationed at Cantonment Gibson! That's Indian country, George, *real* Indian."

The brothers cheered.

As soon as he was settled at his new post on the western frontier of Arkansas, Julius began to send excited letters to George. The West was wonderful, all they had hoped, but the Indians were growing hostile. Any expedition must be expensively outfitted and protected. Save money, Julius urged, and in a year or two they could go West together in proper fashion.

George worked even harder. Money flowed in faster as his career picked up steam. His dramatic Erie Canal pictures won him a medal; in May of 1826 at twenty-nine, he was elected as an Academician of the New York

Academy of Fine Arts, now known as the National Academy of Design.

Orders began to pour in. Few of them paid more than forty or fifty dollars, but one large portrait of Clinton earned six hundred dollars.

George joyfully embraced success. How else could he solve the money obstacle to his cause? Yet success, most unexpectedly and subtly, was itself a formidable obstacle.

He had committed himself to a venture that was bound to be dangerous, full of hardship and discomfort, and hightly doubtful as to monetary return.

But now, if he chose to pursue the life of a society painter, he could have a lifetime of growing ease, luxury, and general approval. He would be safe, secure, comfortable, prosperous—everything a sensible man could desire. He could court the lovely dark-eyed Clara Gregory, of Albany.

George stared hard at success and practicality, and fought them both. It was much harder to fight Clara's haunting eyes.

While wealthy men waited their turn to sit for him, he visited western New York to paint Red Jacket. The condition of the famed Indian shocked and depressed him. Aging, often drunk and despairing in the prison camp that was called a reservation, the once noble Seneca showed only traces of his old pride and defiance.

This first painting of a despoiled Indian sharply reminded George how remote his dreams still were, of painting unspoiled Indians.

As the seasons passed with the project no closer, Julius fretted impatiently at Gibson. Finally, he resigned his commission and headed East. He found George bogged down with so many commitments for portraits that he could not possibly soon leave on their project.

Seeing his brother's despair, George earnestly assured him that he would clear away the work, and then—

"It's got to be soon or never," Julius said doggedly. "There are moves on now to shift all the eastern Indians west of the Mississippi. That will change things plenty. In a few years settlers will push into the plains, and our chance will be gone forever."

While George agreed, he gestured at his painting of Red Jacket. Its simple, bold strokes spoke of bitter defiance and faded power. Its style, fittingly, was much harsher than that of his smooth portraits of the wealthy. "What if all my Indian paintings are as badly received as my Red Jacket? People think it's crude and ugly. I simply wanted it realistic and honest."

"Bah!" said Julius, and gave his brother a playful punch. "It's fine! Now that Easterners have wiped out most of their Indians they're getting sentimental about them—they want wishy-washy fairy-tale paintings. But don't you give it to them!"

"No fear," said George. He hesitated. "There's another complication, Julius."

"Oh?"

"The name of the complication is Clara Bartlett Gregory."

"Oh!"

"She's very young, and she has delightful black ringlets," George went on dreamily. "She has a perfect profile, a gentle voice, and is a wonderful conversationalist

—that is, she lets me talk about Indians hour after hour, with never an interruption!"

"Perfection," said Julius. "But—"

"No buts," said George. "I know—how can I possibly follow through on our plan and still have a wife? Well, I don't know. But I'll do it." Shamefacedly he displayed some watercolor sketches. "Cupids. I waste hours painting these and writing verses, when I should be painting Indians. I waste money on fine clothes that I should be saving for our expedition. It's awful, but that's what Clara does to me." He turned the cupids face down. "But don't worry, we'll work it out."

He draped his arm fondly about Julius's shoulder and took him off to meet Clara. "And mind, when you tell her of the Indians you met, emphasize their fine peace-loving qualities. She's afraid I'll lose my scalp!"

Worried or not, Clara Gregory was in love with her handsome, energetic suitor, who never tired of explaining his plans for the great museum of Indians. Her father, a rich Albany accountant and real estate owner, could not disapprove of a young man with such influential friends as Clinton and Stone.

In the spring of 1828, buoyed by word that twelve of his paintings and drawings were being exhibited in the American Academy of Fine Arts, George pressured slow-paying clients for money enough to buy a simple ring and brown frock-coat suit with fancy waistcoat. In early May the wedding took place in Albany's St. Peter's Episcopal Church. He was thirty-one, and Clara was only twenty.

The joy his lovely bride brought to George was increased by Julius's frequent presence in Albany. Bubbling with plans for the future, Julius displayed souvenirs from the West and lectured the newlyweds on its wonders.

The trio sailed on gay river parties. They piled into gaudy red and yellow coaches to visit nearby Indian reservations; they tramped arm-in-arm through the Albany Museum, and down green country lanes.

A long happy summer passed, its cicada-droning evenings of lemonade and hand-holding on the porch of the big Orange Street mansion lightened by the merry laughter of Julius.

Even on his honeymoon Catlin found time to paint a copy of a Clinton portrait for the Franklin Institute of Rochester. On a warm September day Julius delivered the finished picture. Planning to sketch the nearby Genesee Falls, he swam out near a whirlpool for a view of the cataract from below.

The golden summer came to a shocking close.

A lounger on the bank heard a muffled cry: "Help! For God's sake, help me!"

The cold water sucked the cheery ex-lieutenant down. Julius Catlin was drowned.

The tragic news sickened George. In his grief he tossed through sleepless nights, tortured by echoes of his brother's last appeal. His dark complexion paled, he coughed heavily, and lost so much weight that his doctors shook their heads and muttered of consumption.

Frightened by his rapid decline, Clara bundled him off to visit the Oneida and Tuscarora reservations, in the hope of restoring his zest through contact with nature and Indians.

42

The degradation of the tribes merely added to his depression. No unspoiled children of nature, these, but poor victims of civilization. It saddened him to paint even the most fortunate of them, such as Chief Bread— half-white, with the polished manners and perfect English of an Oxford graduate—and the Mohegan John W. Quinney, a frock-coated Christian missionary. These were not the Indians of his dreams.

His cough persisted. Fleeing the winter late in 1829, they went to Richmond, Virginia. Old friends pressed them to join their lighthearted round of parties and balls, but George rejected all society to concentrate on the ambitious task of painting 115 delegates assembled there to frame a new constitution for Virginia.

When even this challenge failed to stir him, Clara spoke up. "Julius has been dead a long time now," she said gently. "You mustn't brood forever over him. Or over the loss of your great project—"

"It's not lost," George said crisply. His eyes flared. "No! More than ever, I mean to carry it through. But time—*time* is stealing it away from me!"

Her smooth brow crinkled in perplexity.

"Time," her husband repeated. "Julius was right. Congress is drawing up laws to shift the eastern Indians across the Mississippi. Once they mingle, the prairie tribes will never be the same. And steamboats and railroads will soon do their share. The emigrants of Europe will flood over the prairies, drowning the Indians like so many rats!"

"But you're not well. Dear, you have never been strong—"

"I'll get well," he said firmly. The scar on his cheek

flamed with sudden passion. "I'll *make* myself get well!"

But in this winter of ailments it was Clara herself who was struck down, by the dreaded "intermittent fever" of the tidelands. A kind neighbor patiently nursed her through the crisis, while George took long desperate hikes across the bleak tobacco fields, praying for his wife's safety, and wrestling with an inner conflict.

Once Clara was out of danger, he gratefully painted a charming miniature of the faithful volunteer nurse— Dolley Madison, who had been known as the Belle of the White House during her husband's terms as fourth president of the United States.

And then Catlin faced up to his problem.

The first tender blades of spring were greening the land. If he did not act quickly another precious year would slip by. The cruel decision must be made. Now.

The obstacles to his cause had been many. One by one he had defeated them. He had labored endless hours to overcome inadequate painting technique; he had scurried all over the northeast to make money. He had fought the lure of a silk-cushioned life; he had fought his grief.

Now nothing stood between him and his cause but his deep devotion to Clara.

She was strong enough to sit up in bed now. Soon they would head north, where she could settle down comfortably in her father's house for the long convalescence. He should be at her side, but—

When he took her hand she flinched from the resolve in his eyes.

"I am going to Washington, Clara," he said quietly.

"I plan to get letters of introduction to people in St. Louis."

Her eyes shone with tears. Her voice broke as she said, "Of course, George. You must."

Now as always Clara unwaveringly supported Catlin in the chief purpose of his life. Others were less understanding. Cries of protest rose from horrified friends and relatives.

In spite of the Lewis and Clark expedition of almost a quarter-century before, the land west of the Mississippi still seemed as remote as the moon, a mysterious and hostile desert. Travel was so difficult and perilous that only a handful of traders and trappers for the great fur companies really knew the West.

A man must be insane, they cried, to desert a beautiful young wife, to chuck aside a career sure to bring him fame and fortune—just for the sake of a few greasy redskins who would probably fill him with arrows!

George Catlin would not be swayed.

Years later he wrote: "I tried fairly and faithfully, but it was in vain to reason with those whose anxieties were ready to fabricate every difficulty and danger that could be imagined, without being able to understand the extent and importance of my designs, and I broke from them all—from my wife and my aged parents—myself my only adviser and protector."

In the spring of 1830 George Catlin stood erect and eager on the deck of a packet boat approaching St. Louis, gateway to the land of the prairie Indian.

All the world seemed to quiver in excitement. The row

45

of boilers in the bow vibrated the deck under his feet; he himself trembled like a leashed hound straining for the chase.

At last the great adventure was about to begin.

A Family of Knisteneaux (Crees)

Omaha Warrior

5: The Red Headed Chief

As THE packet neared a wharf on the busy cobbled water-front, George Catlin sniffed, then wrinkled his nose. "Ugh!" he muttered. An overpowering stench rose from the big gray and yellow stone warehouses of the fur companies.

Fur was the main reason for the existence of St. Louis. From this hustling town rugged men trekked into a vast wilderness in quest of beaver and other furs for the savagely competing fur companies. Many lost their scalps, but a few bosses back home got rich.

More powerful than the richest fur baron, however, was the Red Headed Chief.

Speculating on his all-important meeting with this ruler of the West, Catlin thumped down the gangplank.

47

Trim and erect despite the weight of his big bag and thick portfolio, he pushed anxiously into the boom town.

The growth of steamboat traffic on the Mississippi was revolutionizing St. Louis. Acres of high-stacked paddle-wheelers smoked away along the waterfront, dwarfing the older craft—muscle-propelled pirogues, mackinaws, keelboats—still necessary for the treacherous Missouri. The air resounded with sawing and hammering. New wharves were creeping into the river; new warehouses bulked skyward.

In the central marketplace, blanketed Indians mingled with mustached Frenchmen, buckskinned trappers, swarthy voyageurs, and bewildered immigrants. The jabber of English, French, Negro, and Indian dialects was sweetened by fragrance drifting over walls that hid the manicured gardens of the rich old French fur traders who had founded the town.

Rich or poor, Catlin thought nervously, all were ruled by William Clark, co-leader of the famous Lewis and Clark expedition of 1804–06, and known to Indians since then as the Red Headed Chief because of his ruddy skin and red hair. His great exploration up the Missouri and across the Rockies to the Pacific had led to the first solid information of that immense region.

Mentally rehearsing an eloquent request to Clark, Catlin registered at a cheap hotel, and hurried on to the Indian Office.

As a Brigadier General, a Governor of Missouri Territory and now as Superintendent of Indian Affairs, Clark had spent most of his sixty years in contact with Indians. He knew them and liked them. Wielding the might of the United States government with wisdom and good will, he was the Red Headed Chief to every tribe of the western territories. No white man could trade or travel in Indian country without Clark's permission. He gave the government licenses—and he could take them away.

In his crowded waiting room sat proud chieftains who had traveled thousands of miles to confer with Clark. Side by side with the painted redskins they planned to plunder, were wealthy fur traders and hard-eyed adventurers. Catlin presented his letters of introduction to a clerk, and sat down near a grizzled white man.

"Big money in savages," the stranger said confidentially. "The fools go crazy for firewater. For a gallon of whisky they hand you fifty dollars in beaver!" The man smacked his lips and cackled. "Don't have to be good whisky neither. Throw terbaccy or red pepper into cheap alcohol for flavorin', and they'll swill it down."

Catlin's blazing contempt silenced the stranger. The artist rose and sternly removed himself to another part of the room.

When he was at last admitted to Clark's office, a grizzly bear of a man shambled forward to give him a knuckle-squeaking handshake. Still tall, burly, and heavy-browed, the famed Red Headed Chief was now silvery gray.

Clark coolly appraised the artist. "Your important friends back east may admire your talent and your project," he said gruffly, "but I'm a very busy man."

The artist hastily untied his portfolio of sketches and oil portraits of Oneidas and Senecas. In Clark's earthy presence the carefully planned flowery phrases seemed

49

foolish. Catlin spoke simply and earnestly of his determination to paint the still untouched tribes of General Clark's domain.

The general studied the paintings, his face so impassive and stony that the artist's heart sank.

"What do you want from the government?" Clark asked curtly. "Money? A private escort to make you safe and comfortable?"

"No money, no favors! I pay my own way; I can sleep on the ground. All I want is permission to travel and to paint Indians."

"And if you don't get my cooperation?"

Catlin stiffened. His eyes challenged the general's. "With or without official cooperation," he said slowly, "I mean to carry out my design."

"Good," said Clark surprisingly. A quick sunny smile lightened his face. "Your work is good, too," he added amiably. "And your plan—your dream—by George, it's something after my own heart!"

He guided the relieved young artist past deerskin curtains into his private museum. Its walls were crowded with medicine bags, papoose cradles, bullhide shields, lances, bows and arrows. The Red Headed Chief not only ruled Indians; like Catlin, he was fascinated by them.

"Too much like whites," Clark said, indicating some crude portraits of Indians. "Takes a real feel for Indians to paint them as they are. Judging by your work, son, you can do it." From under shaggy brows his keen old eyes appraised Catlin. "Before you traipse into Indian country, though, we'll see how you fare with the Indian delegations that come in here every day."

50

Catlin nodded happily, eager to meet the test.

The next day he was waiting at an easel in the parley room, when a solemn Indian delegation filed in to greet Clark and his secretary. General Clark introduced Catlin, and displayed some of his portraits.

"Ah-ah!" exclaimed the Indian chief wonderingly. The Indians glanced in awe from the portraits to the artist. Making such images was strong medicine indeed.

Catlin's handshake was firm, his smile warm but dignified. With a courteous gesture he indicated that the Indians should proceed with their business. He picked up a brush, dipped it into a smear of raw umber oil paint on his palette, and poised it commandingly above the canvas on the easel.

Although he acted with an air of confidence, he was acutely aware of the suspicion in the dark alien eyes—and of the fact that Clark was judging every move.

The chief hesitated. Like all tribal leaders who came to St. Louis to complain of treaty violations, he wore his most colorful plumage. His long black locks gleamed with bear grease; his face glowed with paint. What a magnificent model! Catlin thought, and his hand tightened on his brush. *If* he lets me paint him!

Perhaps these Indians could not understand what he wanted, with his brush and paints—but at least they must realize that unlike most white men he did not seek their land, buffalo, furs, or scalps. Somehow, Catlin hoped, they must sense the all-important truth: that he was a friend.

The dark eyes seemed to pierce into his very soul. Then, suddenly, the chief made his decision. He nodded gravely at Catlin, turned to Clark, and with a broad sweep of his beaded calumet pipe began to orate. He spoke in long flowing phrases, pausing now and then while the interpreter reduced his prairie poetry to humdrum English. The artist exultantly raced his brush over the canvas. He had been accepted!

Each delegate orated at great length, extended by the need for translations. Thus they held poses long enough to satisfy a fast-working artist such as Catlin, who quickly captured likenesses.

At the close of the parley the Indians filed out, and Clark inspected Catlin's work. He grinned at the excited artist.

"I knew you could handle a brush," he said. "The knack of handling Indians, though, is a sight rarer. You're welcome to return any time, Mr. Catlin."

For many days thereafter Catlin worked diligently in the parley room. A growing friendship with the Red Headed Chief resulted in long evenings of yarn-spinning and swapping of Indian lore. Through Clark, Catlin met many important people, including Clark's own nephew, Major Benjamin O'Fallon.

The dashing major had power, as an Indian Agent, and wealth, as the husband of a rich woman. Frontiersmen respected him as an expert duellist, a connoisseur of whiskey and a breakneck horseman. Society respected his courtly manners, cultivated air, and appreciation of the finer things of life—such as good paintings.

Like his uncle, Ben O'Fallon was fascinated by Indians. His palatial house, Indian Retreat, eventually held a fine collection of Catlin paintings.

"This is your Western home," he told Catlin. "When you travel, store your gear here. When you get lonely for that pretty little wife back in Albany, drop in. We'll cheer you up!"

The artist's eyes clouded; sorrow stabbed his heart. Not even his closest friends would ever know how desperately he missed Clara. How could they? All they saw was a lively man, sunny and optimistic, happily obsessed with the pursuit of Indians and paintings. A man who freely spun out yarns of hunting and fishing but who doled out details of his family life as if they were too precious to be shared. They never saw the forlorn man glooming through long lonely nights in a shabby frontier hotel room, squinting by candlelight through endless re-readings of letters from Clara and scratching out thick letters in reply. Her letters turned to precious greasy tatters in his pocket—but paper was a poor substitute for the touch of her soft hand in his.

Clara was well again; she understood his mission and approved—these were Catlin's consolations. Sometimes not only a man but his wife as well, they had agreed, must sacrifice for the husband's cause. He and Clara understood the price that must be paid, and they paid it without hesitation. But there were solitary hours when each mourned the cost.

Although Clara was comfortable in the home of her rich father, Catlin proudly emptied his meager purse every now and then to send her money. Meanwhile, noting his threadbare clothes, General Clark had quietly spoken to prosperous St. Louis citizens.

"A most excellent artist," Clark would say. "And

available to paint a portrait. You'd look fine on canvas, Sam—an important man like you!"

And Sam, or George, or Pierre, would usually take the hint from the most powerful man in the West. Besides, Catlin's only competition came from an armless woman who cut out profile likenesses with a pair of scissors held in her mouth!

Catlin rushed through these bill-paying commissions, impatient for his real work of painting Indians. He yearned to escape the city completely, and to sketch Indians in more natural surroundings. But until Clark gave the word he was chained to St. Louis.

He painted a portrait of William Clark—and refused to take payment from such a good friend. He painted another of General Winfield Scott, a remarkable six-foot-five giant, so bursting with strength and vitality that he could scarcely sit still before the easel. Famous for the Battle of Lundy's Lane in the War of 1812, when two horses had been shot out from under him, Scott was a leading general on the frontier.

Catlin, who occasionally took a glass of wine, but was temperate both in eating and drinking (he never smoked, except the ceremonial Indian pipe), warmed to the hero's denunciation of liquor.

"I have a standing order, Catlin. Any soldier found drunk must dig a grave his own size and contemplate it, with the understanding that he will soon be filling it if he keeps on drinking!"

Catlin laughed approvingly. If only the Indians had such a battler for temperance to protect them from the white man's firewater!

54

In preparation for his first field trip, Catlin soaked up knowledge of Western Indians. Almost every male, he learned, was a soldier. A brave was one who had fought, but without taking a scalp or killing an enemy. To become a Warrior an Indian must take at least one scalp.

"Indian names are confusing," Clark told him. "A man can have several different names. He might lend one or give one away. On great occasions he may even change his name. And there's no written language to make things orderly!"

Catlin sighed. No matter how carefully he tried to identify his portraits he would surely make errors. It was the kind of problem that Clara could have helped him meet, if only the frontier were not so rugged and she so frail.

A vision of her dark eyes rose before him. He could almost hear her gentle voice as he thought of her patiently awaiting his return. Suddenly he knew that the most important day of his expedition would be the day that he arrived home. Not until Clara shared his pride in his work would the labors and sacrifice make any sense.

Months later, in late autumn of 1830, that great day came. His fingertips were specked with splinters from tearing apart bulky packing cases. The racked canvases almost filled a room of the Albany house.

Clara had eyes only for her sun-browned husband in his beautifully embroidered buckskin shirt. Her father, however, impatiently awaited the results of what he considered a crackbrained scheme.

Catlin turned the portrait of an Omaha brave toward

them. "Did this when General Clark took me to the Prairie du Chien treaty grounds," he said.

"Oh!" exclaimed Clara approvingly.

"Humph!" said Mr. Gregory.

Memories flooded Catlin as he glanced down at the thinly painted portrait. The long sail up the Mississippi to Fort Crawford at the mouth of the Wisconsin. And then the Indians! Iowa, Missouri, Eastern Sioux, Omaha, and Sauk and Fox, all thronging the plain, setting up tepees for their long-winded negotiations with Clark. Keokuk, the dignified and crafty old leader of the Sauks and Foxes. Black Hawk, his angry co-leader, threatening war if their people retreated farther west. All kinds of Indians to keep his brush busy—and all kinds of injustice to make his blood boil. Traders cheating Indians with cheap tin kettles in return for high stacks of rich muskrat pelts. Cynical Indian agents taking bribes to let whiskey peddlers into Indian country, and padding the numbers of their tribes to get extra government supplies—for themselves. Villains, most of those agents! Except for rarities like his good friend "Honest John" Dougherty.

"Can't compare with your Eastern portraits," Mr. Gregory said in disappointment. "Crude. Half-finished—"

"Perfectly true," said Catlin. "I worked very fast. These will have to be touched up."

His eyes glowed at thought of how his brush had flown. Mr. Gregory would never understand how different it was from painting in a comfortable Philadelphia studio with an even north light and genteel patrons who would patiently return day after day to pose quietly until the carefully wrought portrait was done. On the prairie you

56

spotted a likely looking chief outside his tepee, quickly set up a folding easel on a rough field while an interpreter or man like Dougherty tried to explain the mysterious activity to the Indian. You set to work at furious speed, racing against time and the inclination of the Indian, while the summer sun smote your scalp and glared fiendishly on the canvas. Mosquitoes whined in your ears, eyes, and nostrils. Flies mired themselves in the blobs of paint on the palette. Curious half-wild dogs sniffed and chewed at your bootlaces. Indian urchins giggled, pressed close enough to menace the easel.

No, these were not finished studio portraits! No time here for subtlety and softened edges. You slapped the oil directly on the canvas to catch a likeness with thick bold strokes. You held back the curious onlookers with dignity, an intent gaze, and a fierce tight-lipped concentration on the job at hand. And always there was a sketch-pad ready in your pocket. To catch the action of whirling dances and galloping hunts you jotted down quick rough sketches in pencil. Later, with scores of these hasty notes to consult and the details still fresh in mind, you painted the scene on canvas.

Hard work—but out of it had come approval from Clark for another jaunt, this one hundreds of miles up the Missouri to Cantonment Leavenworth.

"How elated you were to be going there," said Clara, recalling his letters. "And how depressed when you got there!"

Catlin's mouth twisted wryly as he displayed paintings of the Kickapoo, Potawatomie, Weah, Peoria, Shawnee, Kaskaskia and Delaware. All calico tribes, these—miserable displaced people from the East. Refugees in their own land, toying at farming, loitering dismally about the cantonment, decaying before his very eyes.

Like the pitiful old Indian in a brass-buttoned frock coat, hobbling toward him with open palm extended. A noble people once, but beggars now. Or drunkards. Or clowns, like the strutting brave in a derby hat still wrapped in brown paper and green string. Willing models, yes—but Catlin craved wilder, prouder game.

"Who is that sour chap?" said Mr. Gregory, pointing at the portrait of an unhappy Indian with long feathers in his pierced ears, and a ring in his nose.

"Ten-squat-a-way, a famous Shawnee chief," Catlin said shortly.

Like his famous brother Tecumseh, Ten-squat-a-way had tried to unite all Indian tribes into an army to repel the advancing whites. His eloquence rang chimes of patriotism from border to border. A great army rallied as he brandished secret weapons of magic and mystery, his medicine fire and his sacred string of beans, that would sweep away the arrogant white intruders. United for once, perhaps the Indian armies could have turned back the invaders for good. However, jealous Indian foes challenged the power of his medicine—and Ten-squat-a-way could not make good. Any Indian whose medicine failed lived thereafter in disgrace. The armies melted away, ashamed of their crushed leader.

Catlin stared sadly at his portrait of the forlorn, half-blind chief. One more defeated remnant of past glory, he thought. A symbol of all that he had yet seen of the West.

58

His frown vanished as Clara touched his arm. "Are you satisfied?" she said.

"Well, it was wonderful," he said slowly, recalling how William Clark had ridden out from Leavenworth with him to Konza country. The stalwart old general in buckskins and coonskin cap, the artist in a new leather jacket and visored hunting cap, riding westward over the undulating sea of grass.

Packs of dogs yipped out of the dusty brown Konza towns to greet them. The Konza warriors wore scalps and bear claws. Their scalps were painted blood red, and shaven clean except for one braided scalplock. Why that one remaining tuft? A point of honor. It was an offering to the enemy, if he could get it, as a battle trophy. Only a coward would shave off the scalplock, and leave nothing for his enemy to grasp.

"The Konzas were almost wild," Catlin said to Clara, and again his lips twisted wryly. He gestured at the bold Romanesque profile of his portrait of Wa-hon-ga-shee, No Fool. Only his own stern concentration and Clark's authority had kept such Indians under control while he painted. "But some of them wore horn-rimmed spectacles!"

When chill winds rustled the browning prairie grass, Clark had led the way back to St. Louis. A few quick portraits to raise funds, a few gay evenings with the O'Fallons and the Red Headed Chief, and then the artist was homeward bound. A thrilling summer, he thought; and a frustrating summer.

Clara still awaited his reply.

"I was happy," said Catlin, "but not satisfied."

He saw the sudden concern of Mr. Gregory, and Clara's effort to conceal her sudden fear. How could he make them understand?

"The Indians I saw have been too much with the white man," he said. "They're changed from their natural state. But there's a place, thousands of miles up the Missouri where the Crows and Blackfeet are still in their natural state. They're untouched, unspoiled, undefeated. They don't know their days are numbered." ("The odds are against you," Dougherty had warned him. "You'll never get there.")

"I mean to go there," Catlin said firmly.

Mr. Gregory flushed. "To waste more years in the wilderness?" he cried angrily. "To lose your scalp? To make my daughter a widow?"

"No fear," Catlin said. He reassuringly put his arm about Clara's shoulders, and gave her a comforting hug. "The real danger is on the edge of the Indian world. The farther I go into that world, Mr. Gregory, the safer I'll be."

"Preposterous!"

"Not at all." Catlin warmed up to his favorite theme. "Naturally Indians who have been cheated and mistreated by whites—as they are on the border—are dangerous. But the Indian in his natural state, still secure and unharmed by whites—why, I'm sure such an Indian is perfectly harmless!"

Mr. Gregory snorted in disgust. "The wilder they are the tamer they are, eh? You may pay with your life for such an idiotic faith!"

"I think not," said Catlin. He turned to Clara, his

60

only real worry. The hazards, labor, expense, and scorn of others did not bother him. But Clara, patiently waiting away the long months while her husband pursued a dream over the prairies, what of her? "Do you object to my return, dear?"

She stood stanchly at his side. The fond squeeze of her hand against his, and the soft proud look in her lustrous eyes, gave him the answer.

Ten-squat-a-way, The Shawnee Prophet

La-doo-ke-a, The Buffalo Bull

6: *Plans and Pawnees*

THE MONTHS of work and travel with Clara that winter were so sweet that Catlin wondered how he would find strength to tear himself away.

Clara was at his side when he drew views of Niagara Falls on flat, specially prepared lithograph stones. Later she watched him color the prints made from these stones for publication in a little book. She exulted at the ready sale of the small watercolors of Indians he dashed off from his field sketches. She exclaimed over his skill in painting a delegation of Menominies visiting Washington, D. C.

Their happy talk of the family they hoped to have some day was cut short in the spring of 1831.

"Dougherty is waiting," Catlin said uneasily. The upright Indian agent had promised to take him on a jaunt over the prairies into the Indian territory of the Platte River.

"Don't worry, Clara," he said hastily, as tears welled in Clara's eyes. "It's safe. I know it is. Why, the Indians will be so harmless that I wouldn't hesitate to take *you* along! But the real hazards for a delicate thing like you are in nature—sleeping on the ground in rainstorms, riding all day over prairies baking in hundred degree heat, drinking scum-covered water, fighting off ravenous clouds of mosquitoes—"

"I know you're right, George." She bit her lip, and tried to smile. "But you must let me worry. Just a little!"

He brushed away her tears, and departed. It hurt to leave Clara—and yet as he neared the prairies his pulse quickened, and his spirits soared.

He found St. Louis buzzing about the *Yellowstone,* hopefully designed to be the first steamboat to navigate the upper Missouri. Until now travel up the unruly Missouri had been incredibly tedious. Its floods and shallows, rafts of floating trees, shifting currents, and sandbars that appeared and disappeared overnight, had defied the steamboat.

Large parties and sizable cargoes depended on clumsy sixty-feet-long keelboats. To propel them upstream twenty to forty strong men heaved and strained along uneven riverbanks, pulling the cordelle—a line almost a thousand feet long, attached to the mast. When cordelling was impossible, they poled or used oars. The slow backbreaking pace made only one trip a season possible.

"If Chouteau's steamer ever reaches Fort Union,"

said General Clark at Ben O'Fallon's one evening, "the West will never be the same."

Two thousand miles upriver from St. Louis, on the mouth of the Yellowstone River, Fort Union was a fur-trading post deep in untamed Indian country.

"No wonder that foxy Chouteau ordered a steamer for the American Fur Company!" Ben O'Fallon said. "If it works, they can make large-scale deliveries and pickups in the heart of fur country. The competition will fold up, and Chouteau will corner the fur trade. Think of his profits!"

But Catlin was thinking of Crows, Blackfeet, Mandans, and all the other unspoiled tribes that would suddenly become accessible if the *Yellowstone* defeated the Missouri.

"I've got to get on that boat!" he suddenly exclaimed.

General Clark warned that Pierre Chouteau was a tough businessman, diamond-hard beneath his suavity.

"The *Yellowstone* is a daring gamble to make money," Clark said. "Every inch of space on it will be precious on its big try next season. I'll speak to Chouteau—but what profit will he see in an artist?"

Disheartened, Catlin left St. Louis and ascended the lower Missouri to the Platte River, starting point of the Upper Missouri. Nine miles above the Platte was Dougherty's agency, Bellevue, a lovely spot in the midst of productive fields and orchards.

At the welcoming dinner Dougherty discussed their coming trip up the Platte to primitive villages under his jurisdiction, but the artist spoke mainly of Chouteau and the *Yellowstone*.

64

"I'm not one of Chouteau's favorites," said Dougherty, whose caustic reports to the Secretary of War had often blasted the fur trade. "Fur traders menace the Indian. Traders mean liquor, legally or illegally—and liquor destroys primitive people. How can we prepare Indians for what we call civilization? Through firewater, disease, and worthless trinkets, traders make that preparation impossible! While I labor to get Indians to give up the chase and become farmers—their only chance to survive the coming white hordes—the traders lure them away to search for furs!

"Pierre Chouteau may be a fine man at a dinner party in St. Louis," Dougherty concluded angrily. "But here, he is my enemy!"

Catlin gloomily agreed. The traders, businessmen, and agents he met were usually likable men, and his sociable nature kindled to them, but their treatment of Indians dismayed him. He was too honest to pretend to agree, yet too polite to wrangle constantly with them. His course now was difficult. To the extent that Chouteau was a foe of the Indian, he was a foe of Catlin. But only Chouteau could open the gate to a great adventure and the fulfilment of Catlin's cause—which would help the Indian.

Pondering his dilemma, Catlin rode with Dougherty into the Platte country. The prairies were blooming with spring, and overhead vast flocks of parakeets flashed like red and green fireworks.

Although Dougherty's honesty had won the Indians' respect, they rode warily, always on the alert. At night they staked their horses close to the campsite. They had just passed a great salt marsh when Catlin stiffened in the saddle.

"Look!" he cried.

A tawny and naked Oto brave rode wildly along a ridge above them.

The artist breathed in sharply. Would that breakneck rider prove or disprove his faith in the basic friendliness of the untamed Indian?

The two whites rode on. Before they reached the earthen huts of the Otoes, a chorus of frenzied shouts echoed from the bluffs above. Lights glittered from whirling tomahawk blades. Down toward them streamed a torrent of Oto horsemen. Painted vermilion, shaking feathered spears, they raced with terrifying whoops round and round the visitors.

"It's a welcome, not an attack!" Dougherty cried. Catlin nodded calmly. It was only what he had expected.

Once this splendid escort had pranced them into town, Catlin lost little time in painting the more eminent warriors such as No-way-ke-sug-gah, He Who Strikes Two at Once, and Raw-no-woh-krah, The Loose Pipestem. The latter wore a tunic made of the entire skin of a grizzly bear.

The Otoes were a minor group compared to their allies, the Pawnees, who dwelt in four towns farther up the Platte. A few days later the powerful and warlike Pawnees staged an even more spectacular welcome.

An entire hillside swirled with color when thousands of Pawnees screamed toward them. Pawnees wore oriole and cardinal feathers in their scalp tufts, and painted not only their faces and chests, but brilliantly streaked and

66

blotched their sturdy horses as well. They rode like devils in a nightmare.

"Don't be frightened!" Dougherty shouted. With his bad ear to the agent, Catlin could not hear him above the thundering hoofs and mad yells. "Keep calm!" bellowed Dougherty through cupped hands. "Never let them see you're afraid . . ."

His warning petered out with the realization that Catlin was smiling in joy and elation.

"I should have known," Dougherty muttered to himself. "The wilder they are the more he loves it."

In the Pawnee towns, naked children packed the huge rounded rooftops to watch Catlin paint some of his most notable portraits, including that of The Horse Chief, head of the Grand Pawnees, and The Buffalo Bull, whose "medicine," a buffalo head, was painted on his chest and face.

He worked with growing confidence. First the Otoes, then the Pawnees had justified his faith in them. Next came Dougherty's other charges, the Missouris and Omahas—and once again the gloomy warnings of his father-in-law were disproved.

Dougherty thoughtfully watched him paint The Big Elk, a famous Omaha warrior. All was as usual, with a canvas 28 by 23 inches, and quick bold strokes of oil paint for The Big Elk's strange, proud head, with its reddened scalp, its face blackened for war except for a few crimson lines rippled across it. Quickly but carefully, the artist caught the details of the golden-brown robe with its rose lining, the yellow leggings with their beading of red and blue-green. But despite the painter's concentration,

Dougherty thought he detected signs of discontent. Now and then the artist paused, and glanced toward the far northwest with a remote look in his eyes.

"Still aching to get on the *Yellowstone*, Cat?"

Catlin's teeth flashed in a quick grin. "Still aching. And still no idea how to get on it!"

By autumn, preoccupied with the problem, he was back in St. Louis.

Through a friendly young Indian agent, John F. A. Sanford, he painted a party of Crees and Assiniboins en route from the Missouri's remote headwaters to Washington.

"There's the one who interests me," said Catlin, indicating a proud and handsome young Assiniboin warrior. Wi-jun-jon, The Pigeon's Egg Head, the son of a chief, epitomized the elegance of the untamed Indian. He wore a beautiful costume, with leggings and shirt of mountain goatskin, decorated with porcupine quills and the scalp locks of his enemies; a headdress of war eagle feathers; a robe of buffalo-bull skin, decorated with scenes of his battles.

"His great adventure is just the reverse of mine," mused Catlin. "He's the primitive, venturing into the strange unknown land of civilization. He faces unsuspected perils. The Pigeon's Egg Head won't lose his scalp—but will he keep his head?"

Sanford grumbled about the chore of shepherding the Indians on the Eastern tour. How could he court Miss Chouteau from Washington?

"Miss Chouteau?" said Catlin. "Pierre Chouteau's daughter?"

Sanford nodded. He thoughtfully eyed the bronzed artist. "She likes me, but thinks my only friends are lard eaters from backwoods trading posts. If I called with a cultivated Easterner like you—a lawyer *and* an artist—by golly, she might be impressed!"

Catlin's heart pounded with sudden excitement. Worldly wise now from dealing with a wide variety of savage and civilized men, he understood the advantages of a casual request in the relaxed atmosphere of a home.

"I'll be delighted to help your cause with the fair lady," he said.

"Great!" Sanford slapped him on the back. "Say, will you try to entertain her father—while I try to whisper sweet nothings into her ear?"

"Mind?" Catlin laughed until tears came. "I'll do my best, John. You have no idea how hard I'll try!"

The next evening, in a luxurious parlor befitting the grandson of a founder of St. Louis, Catlin tried to win a place on the *Yellowstone*. His mangled French amused Chouteau, and so did his ideas on the merits and virtue of the Indian in his primitive, untouched state.

"Ah, m'sieur, such romantic notions," said Chouteau. "Your noble Blackfeet are ferocious. Zey scalp my trappers!"

Catlin stood his ground. "After all, their country is being invaded . . ."

Chouteau puffed cigar smoke and listened to Catlin talk of painted savages and painted pictures. At Fort Union, Catlin would at last see Indians in their original, completely untouched state. Think of the value to science and art, Catlin urged.

Occasionally Chouteau chuckled at what struck him as an absurdly sunny appraisal of redskins. He had the sharp unsentimental mind of a born merchant. Although his business sprawled over a million square miles, much of it in unmapped territory, Chouteau carried its every detail in his head.

Only seven years older than the artist, Chouteau regarded him with a mixture of paternal amusement and real interest. Although business came first, Chouteau collected Indian curios and helped scientific expeditions in their researches.

"Your paintings of Crows and Blackfeet would be ver' interesting," he said toward the end of the evening—and cast a keen glance at Sanford, who seemed dangerously close to holding his daughter's hand. "But everyone with zee most petite excuse begs for a ride on zee *Yellowstone!*"

He hurled his cigar into the fireplace, and scowled. "Fools! Eet's no pleasure cruise—just two thousand miles of mud, snags, sandbars, tornadoes, mosquitoes, savages. But zey all plague me!"

"Then I will plague you, too," Catlin said, with affable stubborness. "Please—s'il vous plait—"

Chouteau choked at the accent. "You have a weenning way," he said, chuckling. "And I *would* like to see such paintings." Catlin's hopes soared. "Oui. I'll try to find room, m'sieur. But don't count on it. I cannot tell till just before zee start."

It was a hopeful evening of courtship both for Catlin and Sanford, who eventually married the girl. Catlin returned east bubbling with plans for the future.

"So far, so good," he told Clara. "The record I've

made of Indians is of real value, and I've learned a great deal. But portraits alone aren't enough. I want to paint ceremonies, sports, hunts, everything. And I must keep notes. There must be a written record, too!"

Clara relaxed in his arms. "I'm so glad you're back," she whispered.

"But it all depends on Chouteau and the *Yellowstone*," said her husband. He stared westward through the frosty Albany window. "Will he find a place for me? Or will my project be sacrificed to make room for a few extra bushels of beads and a keg of tobacco?"

Choctaw Eagle Dance

Sioux Buffalo Chase

7: Up the Missouri

BY THE END of January, 1832, Catlin had returned to St. Louis, for the *Yellowstone* was to steam upriver as soon as the ice went out.

He hurried to inspect the new steamer at its riverside wharf. With its 18-foot sidewheel, two smokestacks, and powerful engine, it looked as sturdy as a buffalo bull. In its 130-foot length were carpenter and smithy shops for repairs whenever rocks and snags ripped her paddles or planking. Chanting Negro slaves loaded a cargo of beads, blankets, flints, scalping knives, tobacco, powder and balls, hawk bells, and finger rings.

Catlin frowned at the numerous barrels of alcohol. A new law forbade shipping alcohol into Indian country after July, 1832, and this was the last legal cargo. Since Indian trade was based on getting the customers drunk before bargaining time, however, Catlin expected the traders would try to evade the law.

Toward the end of March, with the river running high and ice-free, Catlin got the long awaited word. He could go!

Already securely packed with rolls of canvas and a folding easel was his case of bladders, plump with their precious oil colors. (Small animal bladders made airtight, though fragile substitutes for metal tubes.) The artist clambered happily aboard with his gear to join a colorful group: the rough engagés of the fur company—tough French-Canadian voyageurs, bearded Yankees, half-breed trappers; Sanford and his returning Indian delegation; the self-assured Pierre Chouteau, impatiently pacing the captain's bridge.

On March 26 the historic voyage began. Crowds waved and shouted from the levee and blazed away with muskets as the *Yellowstone* backed out of her slip into the Mississippi and headed upstream for the nearby mouth of the Missouri. The boat's 12-pound deck cannon and its smaller swivel guns boomed and belched smoke.

In charge of the long battle upriver was Captain Dufond, best keelboat pilot on the Missouri. Before long the passengers joined in the battle. When the *Yellowstone* stranded on sandbars everybody piled out to tug, straining at the cordelles to pull the boat over the shallows. Then the steamer, dodging snags and floating logs, would chug into rapids that swept her back downstream out of control—and then bravely charge forward again.

The banks bloomed with spring. Northbound geese honked overhead, and parakeets circled Catlin and others when they stretched their legs by hiking across peninsulas almost encircled by the snaking river.

At nightfall, or during the riotous rain and wind storms, the steamer moored in inlets. Chouteau's men, alerted by Indian runners, had stacks of firewood fuel ready to feed the hungry *Yellowstone*. The men spun yarns about bonfires on the beach.

John Sanford told of Wi-jun-jon, The Pigeon's Egg Head, the handsome warrior Catlin had painted the previous autumn.

"Wi-jun-jon was bowled over by civilization. He loved it—especially pretty ladies and firewater. He was the first to arrive at receptions and the last to leave. When he shook President Jackson's hand at the White House he began a speech that would still be going on if I hadn't cut it off. He loved New York City, too, and the forts and guns, steamboats, tall buildings, dancing ladies, concerts, parades, balloon ascensions."

Sanford smiled ruefully. "After a winter of being feasted by the Great White Father, Wi-jun-jon was a changed man."

"There he goes now," said Catlin, as a strange figure strutted by, blithely whistling "Yankee Doodle." Wi-jun-jon's beautiful costume of skins had been replaced by a full-dress military uniform with golden lace and shoulder epaulettes bigger than pancakes. Now and then he stumbled over his dangling broadsword. High-heeled boots pinched his feet; a stiff collar rose above his ears. A red feather two feet high jutted from his towering top hat. One kid-gloved hand twirled a blue umbrella; the other fluttered an ornate fan.

74

And from his rear pockets bulged two whiskey bottles.

"Alas for The Pigeon's Egg Head," said Catlin. "His return to the Assiniboins is something I almost fear to see."

Near the mouth of the Niobrara River, in what is now northern Nebraska, the *Yellowstone* stopped briefly at a Ponca village. Beyond this point Indian tribes had not yet been affected much by white men, but the Poncas had suffered bitterly.

Their chief, Smoke, posed for Catlin on the deck of the steamer and quietly related how four-fifths of his tribe had been destroyed by whiskey, smallpox and the dispersal of their staff of life—the great buffalo herds.

Although the herds were still vast, they were retreating from the eastern rim of the prairies before the barking rifles of the oncoming white man. When the herds retreated, tribes that depended on buffalo for existence must retreat along with them.

The Poncas were dismantling their buffalo skin tepees to move west in quest of better hunting. When the dwellings were flat on the ground, Catlin noted a pitiful sight—an ancient and withered man about to be "exposed."

At first the plight of the old man seemed a good subject to the artist. With a sketchbook in one hand and a pencil in the other he prepared to draw this withered bag of bones, who had once been a chief and man of distinction.

As he watched the bent figure mumble words of farewell to friends and relatives, the full meaning of exposure struck him. This man was too feeble to travel— so here he would stay until he died! A cold chill ran through Catlin as he looked at the meager store of fuel— a few sticks of wood within reach of the gnarled clawlike hands. For shelter, nothing but a buffalo skin stretched overhead. For food, a few bones with shreds of meat; for drink, a dish of water. That was all. The old man would sit alone, hunched over, while wolves howled and came closer and closer, and his life slowly ebbed away.

Catlin winced. He moved closer, and looked deep into the sunken eyes. No sign of complaint. No tears, no self-pity. Nothing but infinite weariness and acceptance of the harshness of life.

"My children," the patriarch quavered to his solemn tribesmen, "our nation is poor. You must go to country where there is meat. My eyes are dim, my strength is gone, my days are numbered, and I am a burden to my children. I cannot go, and I wish to die. Keep your hearts stout, and think not of me; I am no longer good for anything."

The way of the nomad seemed cruel, mused Catlin, but when people must travel to live what else could be done with those incapable of travel? It was their way of life, and of death. The grieving relatives left, and rode westward, and the old man uttered not one protest. The artist still remained, staring at the deserted ancient. How long would he sit there, waiting for death? A day? A week?

The Poncas disappeared into the endless prairie. Upstream the waiting *Yellowstone* puffed steam impatiently; its bell sounded. Catlin took the valiant old warrior by

76

his bony hand. Through gestures he tried to indicate his deep sympathy. This was how the Indian race was fated to die, he felt bitterly, alone and starving on the prairie. It was fate, and for all the tears misting his eyes he could do nothing to stop it.

The old man looked dimly at this strange white man—and tried to comfort him with a toothless leathery smile. Once again the steamer's bell clanged.

Catlin wrenched himself away, and ran toward the steamer. Although he had not set pencil to pad every detail was seared into his memory. He would never forget it. He knew he would never paint it either; some things hurt too much to reconstruct, even on canvas.

(Months later, when Catlin came downstream, he found the poles and buffalo skin still standing. Charred firebrands remained a few yards from the skull and other bones, picked clean by wolves.)

The *Yellowstone* puffed, wheezed, and strained on and on through water the color of creamy coffee into wilder and wilder country. Herds of buffalo, elk and antelope scampered in terror from the puffing steamer.

Every detail of nature fascinated Catlin. Often the scientist in him took over from the artist. How heavy, he wondered as he peered into the murky waters, were those giant catfish? He hauled them in, weighed them, and measured them. And the Missouri itself, everybody knew it was muddy, but exactly *how* muddy? He experimentally placed a piece of silver in a tumbler and poured in a bit of the river. "See!" he cried to the loafers on the deck. "A mere eighth of an inch of water makes the silver invisible!" He caught pieces of pumice floating on the river, and pondered on its source. Had this land once been volcanic? What had formed these strange bluffs and strata? What caused mountains to rise, and great lands to sink?

He worked and wondered, while others told jokes and spat into the Missouri.

"Too thick to swim in, but not quite thick enough to walk on," cackled the wits. "So thick it cracks goin' round the bends . . . Ain't enough water to keep the mud wet . . . Yuh got to drink it with a fork."

The eroded bluffs were turning into a fantasy of endless ruined cities with towers and terraces. From early dawn Catlin was riveted to the deck, gazing, sketching, painting. His brush flew over the canvas whenever the *Yellowstone* slowly heaved past Indian villages.

At such approaches the cannons boomed rapidly. Amazed at their first sight of the Great Medicine Canoe, Indians fell down, pressed their faces to the earth and cried aloud. Some sacrificed horses or dogs to appease the Great Spirit; others fled in terror.

If the boat landed, redskins fearfully crept forward to see the fate of their valiant and unenvied chiefs, whose duty it was to board the mysterious smoking canoe. Sometimes the steamer's captain amused himself by scattering them with a sudden blast of steam from the escape pipe.

Although the *Yellowstone* was big medicine, it grounded in low water 200 miles below Fort Tecumseh. While waiting for a rise in the river, Chouteau dispatched a party across the plains to the fort. Catlin took his art supplies and struck out across the prairie with the hardy mountain men.

The treeless plains stretched out before him like an immense sea. Underfoot was lush green turf less than eight inches high, sprinkled with flowers, strawberries, and prickly pear. Overhead hung a sky of overwhelming size.

After miles of hiking in his new Indian moccasins, Catlin sat down to massage his tortured feet. The horizon so neatly encircled him that he felt as if he were centered within a vast, shallow cup—with the tireless trappers disappearing over the distant rim. Determined not to crumple under their cruel pace, Catlin rose and manfully hobbled after them.

At nightfall he finally limped up to their campfire of glowing dried buffalo dung. "When you wear Injun moccasins," they advised him, "walk like an Injun. Toe in."

The next day Catlin tried toeing in, and obtained such relief that within a few days he could stay ahead of the party. From then on he thoroughly enjoyed the trek across a spacious land of strong winds, bounding jackrabbits, and grazing buffalo.

Within a week, on May 23, they reached Fort Tecumseh, soon to be renamed Fort Pierre in honor of Pierre Chouteau. Catlin caught his breath at sight of a big Sioux encampment of six hundred tepees outside the palisaded fort. Dogs snarled and fought by battalions, and thousands of horses grazed on the grassy stretch between the bluffs and the river.

William Laidlaw and Kenneth McKenzie greeted

Catlin warmly. Both were Scotsmen, canny and fearless executives of the American Fur Company. They lived luxuriously in their comfortable dwellings in the heart of the wilderness, and wore uniforms even though the forts were only trading posts.

Quick-tempered but hospitable, Laidlaw captained Tecumseh, the company's key fort in Sioux country. Most populous of all plains tribes, the vigorous Sioux brought in immense quantities of fur and buffalo robes.

Laidlaw's wife, a fine-looking Sioux woman, set a place for Catlin, while Laidlaw arranged a special painting room and promised to use his influence to get good models.

Over fine madeira wine and good food, Laidlaw told how six hundred Sioux had gone hunting a few days before. "They came back in a few hours with fourteen hundred fresh buffalo tongues—fourteen hundred, mind you—and threw them in a hill before me!" He smiled pityingly. "They sold them all for a few gallons of whiskey."

Catlin squirmed. These splendid Sioux depended completely on the buffalo; without their herds they would become as miserable as the eastern Sioux near Prairie du Chien.

"Complete waste," added Laidlaw lightly. "Many skins aren't worth stripping—no fur. And the camp is already loaded with meat. So fourteen hundred buffalo rot away—but Indians will do anything for whiskey."

"Aye, there's your noble savage," said McKenzie slyly. Word of Catlin's partisanship for the Indian had preceded him.

"Whiskey is new to them," Catlin said defensively.

"They regard white men as wise, and able to set the best example—at least in their own customs. I learned to use moccasins by following the Indian way; they expect to use whiskey by following the white man. Since we urge whiskey on the Indian, naturally he thinks it's good!"

The two captains smiled quietly at Catlin's indignation.

"Who is guilty?" cried Catlin. "The simple unknowing savage—or the wise white man?"

"It's only business, laddie," said McKenzie, who headed the Fort Union post eight hundred miles upriver. At thirty-one, his ambition, energy, and leadership made him the company's ablest trader. Although a severe master with little regard for life, he was a splendid host to the select few admitted to his bountiful table. As King of the Upper Missouri, he ruled an area larger than many countries. "Forget the buffalo. They blacken the plains from Mexico to Lake Winnipeg—and always will."

"If the buffalo ever go, the Indian will perish," Catlin said gloomily. "The only hope is the new law banning whiskey. Without whiskey, perhaps the Indian can still adjust to civilization, as John Dougherty hopes."

The captains glanced at each other and remained silent. A wisp of a smile fled across McKenzie's lips.

"Study the Sioux here, Catlin," he said soothingly. "An interesting group. And up at Union, I'll show you even better!"

Catlin lay awake for hours that night, listening to the thump of drums, and barbaric chants and hoots. So many bands of Sioux had gathered to view the heralded *Yellowstone* that an impromptu carnival of dances, religious ceremonies, and sports had developed. It was a perfect opportunity to paint the Sioux and their ways.

Catlin's first portrait of The One Horn, head chief of the Sioux, created a sensation when he hung it outdoors for all to see. The awed Sioux dubbed Catlin "The Medicine Painter." Alarmed by the competition, jealous medicine men denounced the painting.

"Bad luck!" they cried. "Early death for those who give white medicine their bodies and souls." They pointed at the open eyes of the portrait. "They never shut. How can he sleep at night?"

Even the most dauntless warriors began to avoid the blue eyes and wicked brush of The Medicine Painter. Only the words of The One Horn saved Catlin's project. "He is a friend," the chief said of the artist. "He is great medicine. Look at me. Am I harmed? No. And you will not be harmed."

Reassured, the braves gave in to their vanity and curiosity. Prominent chiefs and warriors crowded into the improvised studio to wait their turn. Catlin painted such chiefs as Tobacco, The Black Rock, and The Stone with Horns, a famous orator who bragged constantly.

"It is very easy for me to set all women crying," he said gravely. "All chiefs listen to me carefully before going to war. I am the greatest orator in the nation."

Catlin was also amused by the way each warrior reclined before his portrait from morning till night, admiring his beautiful face, and guarding it from harm. Nevertheless, the artist's obvious respect for Sioux customs won such deep regard that the elderly chiefs turned out to perform the rarely seen Dance of the Chieftains for him.

"It's the highest honor ever paid a stranger," said Laidlaw, a bit startled that a man with such soft-headed notions about Indians could succeed so well with them.

Catlin was working like a man possessed. Apart from the buffalo hunts, ball games, and horse races he painted, there were dances. The Sioux loved dances and seemed to have one for every occasion. In the Bear Dance they imitated the motions of the grizzly. In the Beggar's Dance to the din of pipes, rattles, drums, they shouted appeals to the Great Spirit to open up the hearts of the bystanders to the poor. Most frightening were the Scalp Dances. By the eerie light of flickering torches, warriors hissed, glared, and snarled; they lunged with spear and toma- hawk, and flaunted fresh scalps.

To celebrate the arrival of the *Yellowstone* on May 31, The One Horn gave a great feast. Starting with a graceful tribute to Chouteau, Sanford, Catlin, and the white captains, he added: "We offer you today not our best food—for we have plenty of good buffalo hump and mar- row—but we give you our hearts. For this feast we have killed our faithful dogs. Thus the Great Spirit will seal our friendship."

Catlin's stomach turned queasily as he heard the trans- lated announcement. He sniffed reluctantly at the aromas of the steaming kettles. Savory enough, but his insides rebelled. How could he possibly force dog meat down his protesting throat?

Nervously, his lips pressed tightly together to hide his repugnance, he sweated out the gracious exchange of gifts and lengthy pre-dinner ceremonies. A pipe was lit and reverently presented to each point of the compass and to the sun. After each of the hundred and fifty men had taken the ritual puffs, all in the strictest silence, the dog stew was served in wooden bowls.

Catlin bent over his bowl. Instead of shuddering about the source of these lumps of meat, he told himself, he must seek understanding and try to appreciate the real meaning of the sacrifice.

Beside him a white trapper muttered, "They got good meat, and serve this. The crazy varmints kilt valuable huntin' dogs!"

For a moment the artist was silent, watching a warrior sadly contemplate a dog's head he had fished from a bowl. The Indian's voice trembled as he told how this had been his favorite dog, a wise and fearless friend that had never left his side.

"You miss the point," Catlin said at last to the trapper. "When you have a ton of buffalo meat, and give away a few pounds, the gesture means nothing. But suppose you sacrifice a dog you love, an old friend that you've hunted and fought and played with! Why, that proves that much as you love your dog, your devotion to your fellow man is even greater. Can we whites equal such a gesture of hospitality and friendship?"

The trapper snorted. Catlin picked up his spoon of buffalo horn, and firmly fed himself the dog meat.

An event that same afternoon was more disturbing.

Outside the camp a man was "Looking at the Sun" in an effort to win recognition as a medicine man. Naked except for a breechcloth, the Indian leaned his full weight backward at a 45-degree angle, suspended by a rope running from the top of a pole to skewers driven through the flesh of his chest. Blood trickled from his pierced flesh over the white and yellow clay smeared on his body.

Despite intense pain he had endured this position since dawn, while a crowd egged him on, and medicine men sang, beat drums, and shook rattles in encouragement. If he lasted until sunset he would be cut down, given gifts, and have the prestige of being a medicine man. If he fainted or fell, however, he would be disgraced and scorned forever.

Catlin sketched the scene, and hurried away. Sometimes he felt that the folly of Indians almost equalled that of white men. A tragedy a few days later, touched off by the bad blood between different bands of Sioux, confirmed that feeling.

In his studio tepee, before the usual audience, Catlin was painting Mah-to-tchee-ga, The Little Bear, a distinguished chief of the Onc-pa-pa band. For variety's sake, he was painting him almost in profile. When the portrait was nearly finished Catlin noticed that a surly fellow had entered, and sullenly seated himself on the floor before the subject.

This was Shon-ka, The Dog, Chief of the Bad Arrow Points. Despised by other chiefs, he sat with arms folded, and his lips curled in contempt.

Sneeringly, Shon-ka said, "Mah-to-tchee-ga is but half a man."

Catlin's brush stilled; his nerves twanged an alarm. The chattering Indians were suddenly silent. Nothing moved but the eyes of the chiefs, darting glances at each

other. But Mah-to-tchee-ga said pleasantly, "Who says
that?"

"Shon-ka says it, and Shon-ka can prove it."

The eyes of Mah-to-tchee-ga fixed in burning contempt on the insulting Shon-ka. "*Why* does Shon-ka
say it?"

"Ask the Medicine Painter. He knows you are but
half a man—he has painted but one half of your face, and
knows the other half is good for nothing!"

"Let the Medicine Painter say it, and I will believe it.
When The Dog says it, let *him* prove it."

"Shon-ka said it, and Shon-ka can prove it. If Mah-to-
tchee-ga be a man, and wants to be honored by the white
man, let him not be ashamed. Let him see the whole of
your face."

Mah-to-tchee-ga stiffened. He quietly accused Shon-
ka of ambushing a Sioux and of killing a white man and
stealing his horse. The other chiefs stirred in excitement
as he added, "Mah-to-tchee-ga can look at any one—
and now he is looking at an old woman and a coward."

At this clear challenge The Dog suddenly rose and
stalked out of the lodge, his anger heightened by the
laughter of the chiefs.

The Little Bear resumed his position with a pleasant
nod, and in a few minutes the portrait was finished. Then
he courteously presented to Catlin his beautiful buckskin
shirt, decorated with porcupine quills, a fringe of scalp
locks, and stick paintings of his battles.

In spite of his seeming calm, all sensed a conflict
in the making. Boiling out into the rain after him, the

Indians and Catlin saw The Dog intercept The Little Bear.

"What meant Mah-to-tchee-ga by the last words that he spoke to Shon-ka?"

"Mah-to-tchee-ga said it, and Shon-ka is not a fool— that is enough."

Black as the clouds overhead, The Dog strode violently toward his lodge. The Little Bear entered his, loaded his old flintlock rifle with powder and wad, and dropped a lead ball down the barrel.

In the custom of the Sioux, he threw himself face down upon the earth, and appealed to the Great Spirit for aid and protection. Seeing his agitation, but unaware of its background, his wife feared some rash act and tried to preserve peace by quietly rolling the ball out of the rifle.

Mah-to-tchee-ga's prayers were broken by a harsh taunt from outside: "If Mah-to-tchee-ga be a whole man, let him come out and prove it; it is Shon-ka that calls him."

The wife screamed, but too late. Rifle in hand, The Little Bear sprang through the flaps of his tepee. The guns fired simultaneously. The Dog fled unharmed, but Mah-to-tchee-ga fell into a puddle tinted with his own blood.

Catlin ran to his side, then fell back in horror at sight of the Indian's face. Half of it had been shot away—the side he had left out of the portrait.

Turmoil gripped the camp. Shon-ka's band rallied about their leader, and they raced for their horses as the enraged Onc-pa-pas ran for their bows and arrows and guns. Horses reared and whinnied, dogs howled and snapped at one another in panic, as pursuing Indians screamed for vengeance.

In the chase across the prairie, Shon-ka's arm was broken, but he escaped.

Through it all Catlin stood numbly in the rain. How could he, the lover of Indians, have caused such bloodshed and ferocity?

"It's my fault!" he exclaimed bitterly to Laidlaw, as the dying warrior was borne into his tepee. "I should have had enough sense to stop when trouble was brewing. If I'd painted Mah-to-tchee-ga full face it never would have happened."

"Nonsense. It's his squaw's fault," Laidlaw said gruffly. "And most of all it's Shon-ka's fault. He was sure to make trouble, one way or another. So forget it, Cat!"

The artist shook his head sadly.

Next day Mah-to-tchee-ga died to the pitiful wails of his wife, who blamed herself for his death. But the medicine men, increasingly jealous of Catlin's ceaseless activity with brush and pencil, seized this opportunity to discredit him.

"The Medicine Painter brought death," they said darkly. "His medicine is evil!"

Catlin was too grieved to notice them. Pale with strain, he attended the burial with Laidlaw. He gave gifts to relatives, as well as the tribute of a tepee flying a white flag over the grave. He was too concerned about comforting the sorrowing wife to note the cold eyes of the Onc-pa-pas.

88

"Death to The Dog!" was their vow—but they thoughtfully eyed The Medicine Painter as well.

The tragedy had broken the festival mood of the gathering. It was time for the *Sioux* to return to their home grounds. That day, as Catlin gloomily watched, they lifted their lodges and departed.

"My fault!" he berated himself once more—and even as he did so, his hand began to itch for his sketching pencil. What a fascinating sight this was! Automatically he reached for his sketch pad. Time was too short to waste on brooding. Here, he much catch it all, before it was too late!

At a signal from the chief, six hundred lodges came down flat on the ground. A grand procession of a thousand horses dragged the rolled-up tepees and heavy articles; thousands of women carried infants, puppies, and packs on their backs; thousands of dogs also dragged loads. While the men rode horses or strolled unburdened along the flanks, an entire town crept over the grassy plains.

Before the day ended Catlin had painted and written a full account of the event.

Next day, June 5, the *Yellowstone* also departed.

Wi-jun-jon Going to Washington and on His Return

8: *Fort Union*

UNAWARE OF the mounting threat back in Sioux country, Catlin sailed another eight hundred miles up the Missouri toward Fort Union. Stops were few. Once the high water of early summer receded the *Yellowstone* could be stranded until the following year.

Wi-jun-jon prowled the upper deck, preening for his return to the Assiniboin village just before Fort Union. Although he strutted like a peacock, his uniform was wrinkled and soiled, because he slept in it. His red plume drooped, his fan was broken.

With his blue umbrella raised, and a keg of whiskey in one hand, he stepped ashore before a thousand tribesmen gathered to welcome home the son of their chief.

The Assiniboins gasped at his story of cities, steamboats, stagecoaches, railroads, forts, seventy-four-gun ships, bridges, the wonderful machines in the patent office (a great medicine place), the war parade in New York, the ascent of a balloon from Castle Garden.

"He has been among the whites, who are great liars," they muttered darkly. "All he has learned is to tell lies!"

The *Yellowstone* hurried on, but Catlin later learned the outcome. Night and day Wi-jun-jon told such tales that he soon was regarded as the greatest liar in the nation. His hopes for political power vanished; chiefs shunned him, and only idlers listened to his incessant flow of fantastic facts. While he talked, he tippled. His magnificent outfit disappeared, bit by bit, but he clung to his umbrella, carrying it opened at all times, even on hunts. But as a hunter the once-mighty warrior did little more than strut, drink, and talk about the wonders he had seen.

His lying, Assiniboins thought, was so great that he must have some secret lying medicine. Eventually, after long deterioration, he was slain by a young warrior who felt he was ridding his tribe of a great evil.

The comical aspects of the Wi-jun-jon saga vanished when Catlin heard how a handsome, honest, and once-noble Indian had been killed as a wizard for telling nothing but the truth.

Once again the meeting of white and red cultures had brought tragedy for the red. Catlin wondered sadly whether it could ever bring anything else.

"I arrived at Fort Union yesterday," George Catlin wrote on June 17, 1832, ". . . after a voyage of nearly three months from St. Louis, a distance of two thousand miles. . . . Our approach, under the continual roar of cannon for half an hour, and the shrill yells of the half-affrighted savages who lined the shore, presented a scene of the most thrilling and picturesque appearance."

He lay down his pen and rubbed his weary eyes. McKenzie had generously provided private quarters and a painting room high in a blockhouse on an outer corner of the fort. From its sentry walk he could see a distant landscape freckled with buffalo. Near by were the tepees of a half-dozen tribes here for the summer trading. Their loud chatter and laughter had kept him awake late into the night, but he did not mind. He exulted at being in the heart of the red man's country, where whites were still rare and unimportant curiosities.

"Ho there!" It was the hearty voice of dynamic Mc-Kenzie. "How do you like my place?" He gestured grandly at the palisades of poplar logs and stone bastions. Inside the fort, which ran more than two hundred feet in each direction, were about ten houses and stores. "Fifty men under me. A hundred and fifty horses." McKenzie pointed at the wilderness sweeping toward the Rockies. "Out there is beaver country. That's where the money is, laddie! Blackfeet and Crows, too."

He looked curiously at Catlin's thick letter. "Say! All that for your lassie?"

"This one isn't for Clara. It's for my old friend, William Stone of the *New York Commercial Advertiser*. If he thinks well enough of it, he may publish it."

"Make us famous eh?" McKenzie peered sharply at a clerk dozing in the compound below. Like Chouteau, he was strict and severe in business, yet generous and fair to employees—unless they dared to set up on their own as competition. Then he moved harshly to crush them. But he regarded Catlin as a strange and admirable man, and was always a good friend to him. "I'm trying to wheedle the head chief of the Blackfeet into posing for you," he added.

Stu-mick-o-sucks, The Buffalo's Back Fat, turned out to be a prize catch. With his easel before him, Catlin perched on the cool breech of a twelve-pounder whose muzzle poked through a porthole in the blockhouse, and set to work on the handsome and dignified chief. Acutely aware of the short time he would have in this region of his dreams, Catlin worked at feverish speed—and turned out one of his best portraits.

Out of necessity came a style which demanded quick observation and rapid execution. After a piercing glance at his subject, Catlin roughed in the figure in brown outline. With a few deft strokes he caught the likeness of the warrior or indicated the action of figures in dances or hunts. Landscapes were boldly simplified to the essence.

He painted thinly to stretch his precious paints to the limit. As soon as the canvas dried he removed it from its stretchers and packed it. When he had time he filled in the outlines; sometimes he developed only the head. Later, back in his home studio, he might add finishing touches, but often he let the painting remain in the rough, as if symbolic of Indian life itself.

All that summer he worked at incredible speed. He painted everything that interested him, and he seemed to be interested by everything: musical instruments, prairie vistas, animals, encampments, ball games, a view of the fort, squaws, children, warriors.

To keep track of his growing gallery, Catlin affixed certificates of date, subject, and location to each new canvas, signed by agents, traders, or army officers present at the painting. He hoped in this way to authenticate forever his work, but only one certificate remains.

The portraits of Blackfeet such as The Iron Horn, The Bear's Child, Crystal Stone, The Eagle's Ribs, quickly piled up. Then came other untamed tribes: Crow, Assiniboin, Plains Cree, Plains Ojibwa.

After a day's hard work in the camp, Catlin appeared, as usual, at McKenzie's commodious two-story house, with its glass windows and cozy fireplace. It was like stepping from the Stone Age into modern civilization. He enjoyed the companionship of Kenneth McKenzie, who presided like a feudal baron, and his mysterious right-hand man, Mr. Hamilton. This smiling English dandy, who insisted on a bath every morning and wore the latest London fashions, now clapped his hands and ordered a squaw to fetch a bottle of madeira in a bucket of ice.

"It's the best, old chap," he said. "Frightfully hard to get it up here, but I do. And some fine port, too."

Catlin settled back appreciatively. Hamilton—whose real name was Archibald Palmer, presumably in exile for some wrongdoing—was a storehouse of facts on ancient and modern literature and art.

In the course of a gay discussion of the comic plays of Aristophanes, the famed Greek playwright, Hamilton touched on the religions of that ancient day.

"We mustn't ignore the Indian's religion," Catlin observed, recalling the strange rite that he had witnessed that afternoon, after a Cree (Knisteneaux) had treacherously shot a Blackfoot chief. Following a sharp skirmish which put the Crees to flight, a medicine man hidden inside the full skin of a yellow bear had performed his rites over the dying man.

The crowd about the victim hushed at the approach of the medicine man. His rattles tinkled as he crouched and began his appeal to the Good and Bad Spirits. From the freakish yellow skin dangled the skins of other freakish creatures, and skins of snakes, frogs, and bats, along with assorted beaks, toes, and tails. The freakishness made for medicine, or mystery—something supernatural.

The painted red eyes of the bear glared eerily as the medicine man shook a huge rattle and brandished a medicine spear. For a half hour he jumped, yelped, grunted, and growled like a grizzly in a vain effort to save the Blackfoot. The scene inspired one of Catlin's most powerful paintings.

"Why, the beasts have no religion," said Hamilton. "Not a speck. Don't take them so seriously, my boy." And he launched into an amusing joke relayed from London.

While McKenzie guffawed, Catlin meditated. He rarely confided to the earthy frontiersmen his growing belief that Indians were more consistently reverent than most of the white intruders. The key to their life and character was the medicine bag, a symbol carried by all adult males. Looking to it for safety and protection, the

Indian paid it the homage of long fasts and feasts, penance and sacrifice.

At the age of fourteen or so every boy went alone into the wilderness to fast for as long as four or five days, lying on the ground and appealing to the Great Spirit. The first animal, bird or reptile of which he dreamed was considered the Great Spirit's choice to be his protector through life. After returning to his father's lodge, the boy went on a hunt for the chosen creature. He kept its ornamented skin thereafter, as an object more precious than life itself.

"Ha!" cried Hamilton gaily. "Our talented friend is brooding about red-skinned beasts again. You can tell, McKenzie, by that intense light in his eyes."

"What you need, Cat, is a good hunt!" McKenzie said. "Chouteau is cleaning out my icehouse for the *Yellowstone's* return. What better excuse for some sport? Are you game?"

Catlin nodded eagerly, as Pierre Chouteau and John Sanford entered, just in time to share a good meal of buffalo tongue and beaver tail.

Amused as ever by this eccentric man who saw no need to profit from the Indian, Chouteau said: "Ah, m'sieur, can eet be true? You are returnin' alone in a canoe? Two thousand miles through zee land of savages, all alone?"

It *was* true. Catlin wanted to stop off at Indian villages as long as he pleased, without urgent clanging from the steamer to tear him from his subjects.

"Bon voyage," toasted Chouteau. "May you keep your scalp. Don't forget zat incident of Shon-ka, Zee

Dog. Sioux country is ver' beeg, no? And full of Sioux sworn to keel you!"

Catlin's retort was cut short by a cry of disgust from Hamilton. The dandy's best silk handkerchief had dropped to the floor, and a squaw servant had picked it up and handed it to him. Holding the beautiful silk at arm's length by his fingertips, as if it were contaminated, he marched to the fireplace and tossed it into the flames.

"Beasts!" muttered Hamilton, pale with anger. "Can't bear the slightest contact with them."

Catlin flushed, and clamped his lips tightly together as the bewildered squaw shuffled from the room. McKenzie hastily turned the talk back to buffalo hunts, and the tension soon evaporated. Thought of the next day's hunt excited them all.

Since McKenzie was famed as the greatest buffalo hunter of all, Catlin eagerly rode out with the party the following morning. One of the buckskinned hunters looked a bit condescendingly at the artist, whose pockets bulged with sketchbooks and pencils.

"No time for makin' pitchers on a buffalo hunt," he said. "Reckon you've never been on one."

The artist smiled, and breathed in deeply of the fresh morning air. A light breeze ruffled the prairie grass. His horse trotted skittishly. Already his blood ran faster at thought of the hunt ahead. "I've ridden with the Sioux," he said amiably. "Will you show me something wilder?"

The mountain man grunted, and was silent. Catlin's smile widened. Peerless buffalo hunters, the Sioux rode recklessly on horses trained to approach buffalo on the right side. With bow in left hand, and five or six arrows ready, the hunter shot at the instant of passing, often sinking the arrow shaft clear up to the feather.

Brave men—and brave horses. In the wild chases huge buffalo bulls weighing a ton or so dwarfed the stocky ponies. Sometimes these great bulls sheered off directly into the racing pony, in thunderous bone-breaking collisions. Catlin's eyes only brightened at the thought. Once the fever of the chase hit you—be you Indian, pony or artist—all normal caution vanished. You rode on heedlessly, as if you were indestructible.

Suddenly McKenzie held up a hand, and the party halted, A herd of four or five hundred buffaloes was grazing about a mile before them. McKenzie tossed a feather to determine the course of the wind.

"Everybody strip," he commanded.

Off came any possible hindrance to hunter or horse— hats, coats, canteens, even bullet pouches. Each rider tucked a half-dozen bullets into his mouth, until his cheeks bulged like those of a nut-laden chipmunk. The metal felt cold and heavy in Catlin's mouth. Not even for the chase, though, would he discard his precious sketchbooks.

The men snugly bound their heads and waists with bright bandanas. Catlin hefted his gun, a light and short weapon for ease of re-loading at full gallop. Then McKenzie waved them on. As the party quietly moved toward the browsing herd, the artist felt his experienced buffalo horse trembling under him in anticipation. A tremor swept through Catlin, too. He wiped his damp palms dry, and shifted impatiently in the saddle.

98

When they were still a few hundred yards away the herd detected them. Shaggy heads rose; the beasts stirred uneasily; some of them broke into a trot; others joined them. Slowly they eddied together into a great brown river, that moved faster and faster, and suddenly—

The chase was on! Dust puffed from thousands of pounding hoofs that made a roar like a distant Niagara.

Catlin crouched forward like a jockey on the neck of his flying horse. Rider and horse alike burned with the fever of the chase, straining every muscle to overtake the herd. Even so, McKenzie on his famous pony pulled rapidly ahead.

Catlin neared the herd, passed the stragglers, and then plunged into the midst of the heaving brown mass, his eyes keen and searching. Let others go for cows, which gave the best meat. What he wanted was a trophy—like that giant there whose shoulders bulked mountainously over the others!

Riding at full speed, his wind-burned eyes stinging and watering, Catlin took aim, fired—and promptly lost sight of his prey in a cloud of dust. He reined in his horse and let the herd thunder on. As the roar of hoofs faded in the distance, he found a huge figure materializing out of the settling dust. It was the bull, bristling on three legs. The shot had broken his shoulder.

Catlin whipped out his sketchbook and pencil. This would make the best trophy of all: a series of sketches of a defiant bull! He rode round and round the snorting, crippled beast, pausing frequently to sketch it from different angles.

"I defy the world to produce another animal that can look so frightful as a huge buffalo bull when wounded," he wrote later. "Swelling with rage, his eyes bloodshot, and his long shaggy mane hanging to the ground, his mouth open, and his horrid rage hissing in streams of smoke and blood from his mouth and through his nostrils . . ."

As the sun rose the temperature soared, but Catlin sketched on and on without thought of heat or fatigue. Next to Indians, he felt, there was no better subject than a buffalo hunt. What's more, the paintings he would make from his sketches would give the world its first authentic picture of this American big game hunting. Henceforth—even in the far distant future when buffaloes had vanished completely—the thrilling chase would be visualized and remembered in his terms. All the more reason, then, to do a good job!

His sweat-soaked body was limp with exhaustion, and his right hand ached, when McKenzie and his party returned on their drooping horses. Behind them lumbered five carts loaded with meat. The hunters hooted at sight of Catlin's tough old bull. The artist grinned, dispatched the bull with a shot in the head, and wearily remounted. As the other hunters boasted of their exploits, he and McKenzie remained quiet, for their own deeds needed no inflation. In a daring run McKenzie had killed five fat cows with five shots. A great feat—but not as great as making a dead bull live forever!

Such a hunt called for a feast. The way of man with buffalo meat left Catlin wide-eyed. Into the hungry maws of the camp vanished staggering quantities of fine red meat as choice as the best beef. The company's mountain men, accustomed to a formidable daily ration of six to eight pounds, now ate much more. The hump was highly prized, but some Indians regarded the raw intestines as such a delicacy that they gobbled it down like so much spaghetti. Everybody thrived on buffalo meat. The sickly, feeble-minded and deformed were rarities among these healthy and well-fed plains Indians.

A great boon for the Indian was the buffalo, mused Catlin later as he watched buffalo hides being stored on the *Yellowstone*—but how much longer would the buffalo last? The steamer's capacity to carry heavy loads to civilization would start a new era. Trade would boom in the versatile hides. White hunters would pour in to slaughter the herds.

Others scoffed at Catlin's fears. How could buffalo herds be wiped out? They were as numerous as mosquitoes, and always would be! Catlin was a nice fellow and a good hunter, but why didn't he get drunk once in a while, and stop worrying about Indians!

Catlin held his tongue, watched Pierre Chouteau (on his way to become a great Wall Street financier) depart on the *Yellowstone,* and spurred himself to greater efforts. Surely the *Yellowstone's* epoch-making trip would bring in more steamers, more trade, more white men. The glorious and exciting customs and people of the Upper Missouri were in their last days of untouched security. "Work!" he urged himself. "Hurry! Record it all, before it slips away!"

Now he concentrated mainly on the two principal tribes between Fort Union and the Rockies. These were the savage, black-moccasined Blackfeet (both Bloods and Piegans), and the magnificent Crows.

Although the sturdy Blackfeet willingly traded their own furs to the whites, they resented intruding white trappers so bitterly that they annually slew fifteen or twenty of them.

"Maybe yore safe here," warned one trapper, irked by Catlin's stubborn faith in Indian good will. "But git out of sight of the fort and them murdering Blackfeet will lift your scalp!"

"They might lift yours," said Catlin calmly. "Just as you would kill somebody invading your land and stealing your property. But they won't kill me because I steal nothing, and they know it. I'm a guest, not an invader."

"Just try it," challenged the trapper. "Just go out for a day or two with 'em, and no whites along!"

"I will."

Off he went, on buffalo and elk hunts with the Blackfeet. He came back smiling and more certain than ever that unspoiled Indians would treat whites as friends if they came as friends. Let the cynics and Indian haters shake their heads and call him mad, said Catlin. The fact remained that he placed himself hundreds of times in the power of "savages," and they never harmed him.

"And yet someday," Catlin predicted gloomily, "all this will change." At the moment the Indians of the northern plains were still sure of their mastery of a vast domain. The handful of whites seemed trivial. Feeling no fear, Indians bore no hate. Sitting Bull and Custer were still unborn in the year when Catlin rode alone and unharmed among the Indians, but the grim future was clear to the artist. "Indians are brave men. When they realize that they must fight or perish, there will be terrible wars on these beautiful prairies!"

All the more reason, then, to record tribes like the Crows at the peak of their power.

The Crows were the virile, masculine beauties of the Plains tribes, usually over six feet tall, strongly built, and dressed in gorgeously decorated garments of soft white skin. They were famed for their hair, so extraordinarily long that on some warriors it dragged on the grass as they walked. A chief aptly named Long Hair was the record holder; according to careful measure by two trappers his tresses were ten feet and seven inches long.

Each morning it was the duty of the squaw to groom her warrior's hair, and oil it with bear grease. For ease of carrying, the Crow usually wound his precious locks about a strap, but on great occasions he proudly draped it behind him in a black, shining train.

Although Crows could be valiant fighters, Catlin always found them civil and friendly. Fine craftsmen, their artfully dressed hides remained soft and pliant no matter how often they were wet. Their big skin lodges, often twenty-five feet high and large enough to hold forty men, remained soft and clean even after months of exposure.

Among the Crows Catlin painted were Bi-eets-ee-cure, The Very Sweet Man, and Ba-da-ah-chon-du, He Who Outjumps All. In the latter painting the glory of the Crow warrior is matched in his rearing steed. A bonnet of war-eagle feathers adorns the head of horse as well as rider; the horse's tail floats as abundantly in the breeze as

the streaming tresses of the warrior. The horse, the chief—
and even his quiver and fourteen-foot lance—are richly
decorated. It is the Plains Indian at his peak of pride and
power.

With such thrilling subjects, Catlin painted like a
man inspired. He also wrote letters to William Stone on
the customs of the tribes, and collected craft objects and
curios. Hardly a moment of an entire month was wasted—
and suddenly, it seemed, it was time to say farewell to
McKenzie.

"We'll take good care of your paintings," McKenzie
said, "until the next keelboat leaves for St. Louis." He
hesitated. "I wish you'd let me pay for my portrait."

"Not a chance!" said Catlin. McKenzie had already
bought two Indian paintings at a generous price. "You've
helped a dream come true. It's been everything I hoped
for. Everything!"

Reluctant to part, they walked under McKenzie's
heraldry of a gun and six scalps over the fort gateway.
Catlin's loaded skiff was ready. At McKenzie's urging
he had accepted as companions Bogard and Ba'tiste, both
veterans of the fur trade. Pale from a farewell binge with
their cronies, but tough as mustangs, they waited beside
the skiff.

"Good marksmen, both," McKenzie said. "You'll be
glad to have them. Your love of Indians won't help once
the Sioux or treacherous Riccarees go for your scalp!"

Checking the supplies, Catlin found plenty of ammu-
nition, dried buffalo tongues and pemmican, and a few
dozen beaver tails. Besides his art supplies and some
Indian dresses and trinkets were a few cooking utensils:

three tin cups, a coffee pot, one plate, a frying pan and a kettle. With these meager supplies the trio calmly set out on a two-thousand-mile journey.

Bogard and Ba'tiste paddled from the middle and the bow; Catlin manned the steering oar at the stern. McKenzie, Hamilton, and the Indians shouted as the White Medicine Painter steered into midstream.

"Beware the beast," cried Hamilton. "Don't romanticize them—or you'll bloody well find your scalp flying over some filthy tepee!"

As the fort disappeared behind them, Catlin was silent and thoughtful. McKenzie, Chouteau, Sanford, and Hamilton were the best of companions, and fine men. They were energetic, good-humored, courteous, intelligent, and well-educated.

But Hamilton looked down on Indians as dogs. And John Sanford, his good and upright friend, was something of a fraud about Indians. Now the happy son-in-law of Pierre Chouteau, he put the American Fur Company above his duties as United States Indian Agent. Sanford deceitfully implied to Indians that the government's annuity was actually a generous gift from the fur company.

And what of the vigorous McKenzie and the suave Chouteau? Catlin learned the facts later. While he had been ecstatically painting Indians, Chouteau and McKenzie had been plotting to defeat the new law forbidding shipment of liquor into Indian country. What simpler and cheaper way to do this than to ship secretly an entire distillery to Fort Union? Vats and boilers would be installed. Local Indians would be put to work raising corn and rye for conversion into the whiskey that would corrupt them.

Suspecting some such plot, Catlin despaired. If the best of white men behaved in such a fashion, what hope was there for the Indian?

None.

Although Catlin vowed to fight to preserve the Indian and his way of life, he recognized that defeat was inevitable. His original vision offered the only possible preservation of Crows and Blackfeet in their prime; through his paintings the doomed fascinations of savage life could forever endure.

Even as he swept downstream toward the mysterious Mandans, he fretted, impatient to seize his brush once more.

Keokuk

Catlin Dines with Mandan Chief Mah-to-toh-pa, The Four Bears

9: Mandans: Men of Mystery

THE TRIP downstream began smoothly. Catlin paused often to set up his easel atop the lofty bluffs bordering the river. While he painted landscapes, or studied the eroded strata and theorized on its geological history, Bogard and Ba'tiste hunted.

Game abounded. Thousands of white swans and pelicans flocked where the river swelled into a lake. White wolves stalked wary mountain sheep and antelope. Grizzly bears swaggered through the gullies.

Curiosity caught the fleet antelope. Ba'tiste stuck his gunrod into the ground, capped it with a bright red handkerchief, and then lay in wait. Attracted by the fluttering color, inquisitive antelopes approached so close that even a poor shot could not miss.

Catlin painted these hunts, as well as a vast city of prairie dogs. Inquisitive as any antelope, he inspected the mounds that pimpled several miles of prairie, and made notes on the habits of the little animals.

At night the travelers spread buffalo robes on the grass and slept deeply. One morning they awakened to find visitors. A large female grizzly with two cubs had pawed food and baggage out of their canoe.

With his rifle in hand, and a pair of heavy pistols, tomahawk and a scalping knife tucked under his belt, Catlin felt ready to tackle any bear, but the experienced mountain men tugged him away.

"The rule of the mountain," Abe Bogard whispered, "is never fight a grizzly except in self-defense."

Even with several bullets lodged in his heart, a grizzly could charge on to deal death and destruction. The trio hastily gathered their tattered belongings and pushed into the river.

After two hundred miles of hunting, painting, and yarn-spinning with his boatmates, Catlin sighted a timbered fence eighteen feet high, which walled in the mounded dwellings of the mysterious Mandan tribe. When Lewis and Clark had wintered with the Mandans in 1804–05 they had regarded them as the most remarkable tribe on the Missouri.

Catlin thrilled as he sprang ashore. As the first artist to visit this tribe he felt himself a discoverer. If they lived up to advance notice his most important work would be done here.

A blue-eyed six-foot-two giant shouldered through a crowd of jabbering Mandans and yowling dogs to greet

Catlin. James Kipp commanded Fort Clark, the fur company's Mandan post. In his early forties, he had spent a quarter of a century among Indians, and was perhaps the first white man to master the elusive Mandan language.

As Kipp guided him to his quarters, Catlin noted the Mandans' great respect and affection for him. Here was one of those rare white men, like John Dougherty, who treated Indians as fellow human beings.

Over a bowl of steaming buffalo stew, Catlin and Kipp discussed curious aspects of the Mandans. Why did so many of them have fair skin, and blue or gray eyes? Wasn't it odd that their bowl-shaped boats, made of buffalo hides stretched over a wicker frame, so closely resembled Welsh coracles? Why was gray hair so common, even among the young? How had their strange, secret religious rites developed? No other tribe had a richer variety of games and dances, or built such solid and permanent towns, and yet the Mandans had migrated from some other area—but where? No one knew.

Catlin settled down to write and paint a detailed report of the Mandans. Ironically, the most thorough study he ever made of one particular tribe later exposed him to attack as a liar.

"I have this morning," wrote Catlin, "perched myself upon the top of one of the earth-covered lodges, scalp poles waving over my head, and have the whole village beneath and about me, with the din and bustle of a thrilling panorama."

The rounded lodges of waterproof clay packed over stout timber framework were up to sixty feet in diameter.

Except for the central clearing, site of public games and ceremonies, they were crowded together.

On sunny days, Mandans made full use of their roof-tops. Here plumed warriors gestured and re-enacted battles; there, a lover serenaded with his lute, and laughing groups played the games of "moccasin" and "platter." Sunbathers sprawled idly beside their dogs, among objects such as buffalo skulls, boats, and sleds. Squaws worked on robes and dresses.

Beyond the picket fence Mandans swam skilfully in the Missouri, and in green fields the squaws tended their crops of tiny, thumb-sized ears of corn.

Catlin stirred restlessly. There was so much to learn about this tribe, so much to paint. But, as usual, the medicine men opposed him.

Thanks to Kipp he had already painted the two top men of the tribe, Chef de Loup, and Mah-to-toh-pa, The Four Bears. A great warrior and gentleman, Four Bears was the most popular man in the nation. Handsome, brave, generous, elegant in a robe which depicted his battles, he made a deep impression on Catlin.

The effect of the portraits on the assembled tribe was overwhelming. Many Mandans yelped, stamped out a dance, or wept; some covered their mouths with their hands and were mute; others indignantly plunged spears into the ground, twanged an arrow at the sun, and stomped away.

The jealous head medicine man, Old Bear, played upon the general fear that the artist could make living things by looking at them, and therefore could kill in the same way.

Posting himself outside Catlin's studio door, Old Bear howled warnings of doom to all who appeared. In spite of most fluent persuasion from Kipp and Catlin, only a few brave chiefs dared sit for the artist, and even they quailed before the magic eye and medicine brush.

As he surreptitiously sketched from the rooftop, Catlin decided there was only one hope to save the stalled project. He sent a request to Old Bear to come to his studio next morning. Old Bear appeared, but he was stiff and suspicious.

"I've had my eye on you for several days," said Catlin through an interpreter.

The Old Bear sniffed scornfully, but said nothing. He looked at the medicine—the palette with its bright oil colors—and sniffed again.

"I have been much pleased with your looks," added Catlin hastily, "and have gone to great trouble to learn your story. Everyone says it is most extraordinary, that your character and place among Mandans is outstanding. You above all are worthy of my notice."

Old Bear's eyes flickered uncertainly. He stood straighter; his chest puffed out a bit.

"That is why I have practiced on the others first," Catlin said smoothly. "My hand was stiff from paddling. I had to regain my skill before I felt worthy of you." Old Bear nodded gravely; his eyes flashed proudly, and his chest swelled still more. "At last I feel ready to do you justice," added Catlin. "If we start now, my powers will be closest to matching your position."

Old Bear seized Catlin's hand with a special grip reserved only for fellow medicine men, and he assured

Catlin he had nothing against him, and that his medicine was great. "I would like to see myself very much," he admitted, as they smoked a ceremonial pipe of friendship together, "but the chiefs were many days in this medicine house, and had not asked me to come in and be made alive with paints. My friend, I am glad my people told you who I am. I will go, and in a little while I will come, and you may go to work."

Old Bear took the entire morning to daub and streak himself with paint, bear grease, and charcoal, and to prepare himself with the proper pipes in his hands and fox tails on his heels. A parade of lesser medicine men followed him into the studio. Catlin painted a full-length portrait of Old Bear waving his pipes and singing the song for dying patients.

Thereafter the medicine man preached in favor of the artist's medicine. He lay for hours in the studio before his picture, gazing at it, and shook hands with Catlin a dozen times a day.

The conquest freed Catlin to paint Mandans in their many different aspects.

As swimmers, they excelled. Each summer morning the women frolicked in the river above the village, their privacy protected by armed warriors. Men and boys casually churned across the Missouri, using what is now termed a crawl stroke. Catlin was the first to describe it. Riverside steam baths heated the ill or the winter-chilled with fragrant herb-scented vapors so hot that a plunge into the cold river came as a welcome shock.

As archers, they discharged arrows so quickly that some could put up eight arrows before the first one hit the ground. Like most horsemen of the plains, they used bows only about three feet long.

For entertainment they raced small tough horses, gambled, told stories, played all kinds of games and practical jokes, and danced.

The dead were placed on a platform of poles. When this scaffold rotted away, relatives put the skull in a large family circle of older skulls, all facing inward, on the open prairie. A woman might often visit the skull of her husband or child with food, and chat to it affectionately, as if getting a reply.

As Catlin recorded it all he speculated about the origin of the Mandans. In the Middle Ages a band of men had sailed from Wales under Prince Madoc, and had never been heard of again. Could the Mandans be the descendants of these wanderers? Their light skins and belief in a biblical kind of Flood, their Welsh-type boats and certain similar-sounding words—all this gave weight to the theory.

A man could spend a lifetime studying such people, but Catlin could spare less than a month. His oil paints and his purse were both shrinking. As he impatiently awaited the ferocious annual rites, he sketched, painted, wrote, and studied at such a pace that he overlooked completely his thirty-sixth birthday.

"My conception of the Indian is changing," he told Kipp. "Silent, impassive, emotionless? Ha! These fellows never stop chattering; they love jokes; they love gossip. Why, they're as emotional and excitable as children!"

Kipp agreed. Only by living with Indians intimately as a trusted friend, in Catlin's fashion, could one ever really know them.

Occasionally the artist dined with his best Mandan friend, Chief Four Bears. The artist sat on a decorated buffalo robe spread over a hard earthen floor that almost shone from constant use and sweeping. Sleeping compartments curtained with skins rimmed the big circular lodge. Buffalo robes stretched over pole frames served as beds. Near every man's bed hung a wooly black buffalo head, for use in the buffalo dance.

After ceremonial puffs of the pipe, Four Bears cast a small piece of meat into the fire as a sacrifice, and served Catlin simple but delicious food: a juicy roast of buffalo ribs, a tray of pemmican and marrow fat, and a pudding of wild turnips flavored with buffalo berries. A Mandan chief never ate with his guest, but sat by silently to serve him.

Another pipe was lit after the meal, and the two friends amiably communicated through sign language and pantomime.

"Hell is a place of ice and cold," Kipp explained one morning over breakfast. "If you spent a winter here, you'd know why! Mandan Heaven is a land of warmth, sunshine and buffalo. To please the Good Spirit and appease the Bad Spirit there's an annual four days of ceremony—and torture, or Okeepa!"

Catlin nodded. He already knew the three aims of the rituals: to celebrate the subsiding of the great Flood; to keep the land full of buffalo; to prove the bravery, fortitude and manhood of the young warriors.

At that moment a sudden screaming from women heralded the approach from the prairies of the First or

Only Man. Painted with white clay, robed in white wolf-skins, he related before each lodge how he alone had survived the great Flood by landing his Big Canoe on a mountain peak. Every lodge gave him presents, to be sacrificed into the river so that the Flood would not return.

"It's started!" exclaimed Kipp. "Grab your sketchbooks, Cat. You'll fill them in the next four days!"

Catlin ran to join the crowds gathering to watch the Bull Dance. The fantastic spectacle was almost too complex to grasp. Men under buffalo skins and willow boughs pranced like bulls about a tall barrel which represented the Big Canoe, a sort of Mandan Noah's Ark. Other dancers enacted the roles of Night, Day, and menacing grizzly bears. Rattles shook, and old men chanted and drummed leather water bags. A hundred small boys played the role of antelopes. Everybody was daubed, streaked, and circled with paints, colored clays, and charcoal.

Catlin sketched at furious speed, but new players and bits of action constantly popped up. Fortunately, the Bull Dance was repeated so many times during the four days that he was able to paint an exciting and accurate record of it.

He and Kipp were granted the rare honor of observing the rites within the mystery lodge. While others shouted and danced outside, fifty youths solemnly fasted and prayed for the first three days. On the fourth day—after many thrills outside when a black Devil Man was finally defeated and chased away—the tortures began.

Strange music throbbed within the dimly lit lodge

as the elders prepared to judge the bravery of young men. Weak from hunger, thirst, and fatigue, the candidates stepped forward one by one. A knife, notched to increase pain, was slashed through the skin of chest, shoulders and thighs. Skewers were thrust through the cuts. Rawhide ropes dangling from above were tied to the upper skewers. Then the brave was hauled six feet into the air, all his weight hanging on his own pierced flesh. His quiver, shield, and buffalo skulls were hung from the other skewers.

Catlin winced at the horrible sight. For a moment he averted his eyes, sickened, his sketchbook slack in his hands. Then, gritting his teeth, he forced himself to look again. The bad as well as the good must be recorded about his primitive men.

Their fortitude amazed him. "Several seeing me making sketches, beckoned me to look at their faces, which I watched without being able to detect anything but the pleasantest smiles as they looked me in the eye, while I could hear the knife rip through the flesh, and feel enough of it myself to start uncontrollable tears over my cheeks."

Eerie music continued as attendants spun the dangling men with poles, faster and faster, until agony triumphed over the most valiant. A brave burst into a heart-rending cry to the Great Spirit, then fainted and hung like a corpse.

The youth was then lowered. As soon as he could stir, he dragged his tortured body—still weighted with objects —to an elder with a hatchet and a dried buffalo skull before him. There he rested the little finger of his left

116

hand on the buffalo skull, as an offering to the Great Spirit, and the elder lopped it off.

Enough! thought Catlin. *Enough!* But the testing was not ended. Now the mutilated youth entered The Last Race outside. Two athletic young men pulled him furiously between them, round and round the Big Canoe. While skulls and shields clattered behind him the exhausted youth struggled to endure bravely, on and on, until finally he fell senseless. Then he was dragged still farther, until the weights pulled the skewers out.

The Last Race ended with the circle littered with seemingly lifeless bodies. Each youth was left alone until he made his way home unaided, crawling, reeling, staggering. Once there, though, he was given a joyous welcome. He had won not sympathy, but admiration—for now he was a man. A Mandan man.

Thus ended the rite of Okeepa.

The four days of savagery and sacrifices left Catlin shaken but inspired. He holed up in an empty lodge, under a smoke hole that made a fine skylight, and went over his many rough sketches and careful drawings of what he had seen. With the details still hot in his mind, he made four important and stirring paintings of the diabolic scenes.

Aware that they might stir disbelief, he had Kipp and two clerks sign certificates of authenticity. Aware also of their value to scientists, he wrote careful notes on Okeepa —but was wise enough to admit that he could not explain it all. It was too complex, and his time was short.

After Okeepa, and a frenzied week of putting on canvas the grotesque and monstrous, he longed for a more pleasant interlude. He paddled eight miles upriver with Ba'tiste and Bogard to the Minatarees (or Hidatsas). Their little town on the Knife River was somewhat similar to the Mandans'.

However, the Minatarees were much more warlike than Mandans; they had lost so many braves that the lovely young girls were a vast and lonely majority. They eyed the three strangers flirtatiously. Ba'tiste and Bogard ogled back at them, while Catlin painted their ancient chief, Black Moccasin. The kind old gentleman had befriended Lewis and Clark twenty-seven years before, and asked about Red Hair.

Fortunately for Catlin's strained nerves, the Minatarees were not only at peace but were celebrating their most joyous festival, the Green-Corn Dance. After Okeepa it was a relief to paint this gay scene, and to join in the great feast. Nothing was sacrificed in this ceremony but the first ears of corn—much more to Catlin's taste.

His spirits rose so quickly that he joined the fun of a horse race with the Minatarees. And next day giggling Minataree maidens teased him and his two companions when they tried to cross the river in one of the bowl-shaped bullhide boats. Sleek as otters in the water, the swimming girls spun their light craft about. They tipped it up and down, holding it captive in midstream, while villagers laughed from the shore at the white men's plight. A bribe of strings of beads persuaded the merry girls to release them and laughingly swim away.

But months of constant strain were taking a toll.

"You work too hard wiz zee brush," said Ba'tiste anxiously, as Catlin hacked and coughed before his easel.

118

Never had he and Bogard seen a man drive himself so relentlessly.

"Time is short," Catlin muttered. His head throbbed; fever flamed through his body and glazed his eyes. He daubed more paint on the canvas. "Got to keep going."

He lay down his brush, and picked up his pencil and sketchbook. For a moment the world spun about him. He reeled, then shook his head clear. He pressed his hot dry lips together, squared his shoulders, and strode toward a horse lent him by the Minatarees.

"Mustn't miss the hunt, lads," he said.

Off he galloped with a hundred warriors bent on making a big kill to replenish the town's low meat supply. Each stride of the horse jarred his aching head. He found himself longing for a rest—and sharply reprimanded himself. With a priceless chance coming up to sketch a "surround" only a weakling would give in to a few little pains!

As the Minatarees neared a small herd of buffalo, they split into two columns. Catlin slowed his mount as a wave of dizziness hit him. Suddenly a teeth-chattering chill replaced his fever. He took out his sketchbook and urged his horse forward. To make a good painting of a surround he would need many quick sketches of the details of the action. Somehow, he must ignore his ills.

The two columns of yelling horsemen were speeding in opposite directions to encircle the milling herd in an ever-tightening noose that none could escape. Fogs of dust half obscured the turmoil of galloping hunters whizzing arrows and plunging long lances into the hearts of the great beasts.

Catlin dashed this way and that, jotting quick notes to indicate the wild action. Some hunters, too intent on their prey or blinded by dust, were trapped in the center of the maddened herd. They leaped onto the backs of buffaloes and jumped out to safety, leaving the horses to their own fate. Bulls gored horses and pursued dismounted warriors. Then the fleeing braves would suddenly wheel, snatch a robe from around the waist, and toss it over the horns and eyes of the bull. Darting aside, the hunters then drove an arrow or lance into the bewildered beast.

Within fifteen minutes the savage combat ended. The herd was wiped out. Catlin's pencil dropped from his trembling fingers, but he clung grimly to the sketchbook. Slumped in the saddle, he headed toward the village.

The prairie was a blur about him now, but he jubilantly repeated to himself, "I've got it! Rough as a child's scribbles, maybe, but I'll make a painting from them that will show the world what a real Indian hunt is!"

Ba'tiste little knew or cared whether the stirring paintings of this hunt would become a model used by many later artists in depicting the classic Indian buffalo hunt. He took one look at the sagging, muttering artist and ran forward to catch him before he toppled.

As Ba'tiste eased him down, Catlin burst into a violent fit of coughing. "Great hunt!" he gasped when he could speak. "Wouldn't have missed it for worlds."

Then he collapsed in Ba'tiste's arms.

The trappers took the artist back to the Mandan village, where pleurisy laid him low. Because of his chills he slept on a buffalo robe with his feet to the fire—and a solicitous Indian insisted on offering his bear-greased body as a nightly pillow.

After several days of such unwanted care, Catlin shakily arose and prepared for his return to St. Louis. While Ba'tiste and Bogard stored his precious cargo of paintings and curios on the skiff, Catlin tried once more to buy a beautiful pair of leggings, fringed with scalp locks and garnished with porcupine quills, from a young warrior who had always politely refused to sell.

"I will give you a fine horse," said Catlin, offering a price worth many pairs of leggings.

Again the warrior politely refused to sell.

Catlin shrugged, and turned to the sad business of bidding farewell to good friends. When the noble Four Bears embraced him, the two men were deeply moved, fearing they would never meet again.

Then Kipp's huge hand took his in a firm grip. Catlin thanked him heartily. "It's proved I was right, Jim," he said. "The North American Indian in his untouched state is high-minded, hospitable, honorable—"

"But they're not all untouched," said Kipp. His face was grim as he warned, "Don't stop at the Riccaree village. Pass them at night—and pass fast."

Only a few weeks before a party of trappers had burned two Riccarees to death, and the savage "Rees" were thirsting for revenge.

Catlin sighed. "What a sad change," he said. "Lewis and Clark found the Riccarees very friendly."

"Not any more," Kipp said. "So keep your rifles ready. Don't lose your scalp because of somebody else's errors."

After one more round of farewells, the little skiff was

nosed out toward midstream. And as the current began to catch it, the young warrior who owned the leggings suddenly tossed a parcel into the skiff. Swiftly the skiff rode downstream away from the Mandan village. Catlin opened the package and found the prized pair of leggings.

He turned and waved his thanks to the proud young warrior who stood erect on the bank. The Mandan had carefully waited for the moment of departure, when Catlin could not possibly make any payment for the gift.

Deeply touched by this gesture, the artist found it hard to face the peril ahead. With some Indians so friendly, could others really be on the warpath? Would the Riccarees, midway on the five-hundred mile trip downstream to Fort Pierre, really try to kill them?

Ba'tiste and Bogard smiled grimly, and kept their rifles at their sides.

Catlin Paints the Mandan Chief

Chief Black Hawk and Followers in Balls and Chains
at Jefferson Barracks

10: The Civilized Savages

WITH HIS companions plying the paddles, Catlin steered
down the Missouri past snags, sandbars, drifting logs,
sometimes even through herds of swimming buffaloes.

At sundown they kindled a fire of driftwood under
some towering bluff, cooked and ate supper, and then
floated on for another four or five hours. They slept on
barren beaches, to avoid the maddening clouds of mosquitoes; they slept in darkness, with no fire to attract hostile
eyes. Pistols were at their sides, and rifles in their arms.
They ate buffalo, antelope, elk, and mountain sheep, but
in dangerous areas, where they dared not fire guns, they
fished for catfish.

The rising tension failed to dull their high spirits.
Ba'tiste and Bogard bubbled with jests and tall tales, and

Catlin was their match. Laughing, bantering, yarning, they swept down the Missouri.

At the sight of smoke rising from the Riccaree village in the distance, they suddenly stilled their quips. Instantly, they pulled in under some willows at the shore. As they waited for nightfall, they heard chanting and yelling. In vengeance for the atrocity committed by the trappers, the Riccarees had killed two white men, and were now "dancing the scalps."

Darkness came, but with it a full moon that glared over the Missouri, illuminating each ripple. The trio piled green bushes on top of the boat to give it the appearance of a floating treetop, snuggled low under the bushes, and let the current drift them past the village.

On the bank was a scene to chill the blood. The light of a hundred waving torches gave a clear view of the fresh scalps hung on poles for the nightly Scalp Dance.

Even more menacing than the demoniac shrieks and gestures of the band of dancers were the hundreds of giggling and cackling women who were bathing by the moonlight on a sandbar at the lower end of the village. Catlin groaned silently as the current drifted their craft close to shore. The moon lit the wet shoulders of the merry women—and glinted on the dripping tip of a protruding paddle.

"A canoe! A canoe!" screamed a sharp-eyed girl.

The scalp dancers stopped in mid-song, and raced for their weapons. Torches weaved wildly in the dark, as all sped to catch those who dared try to slip by.

The white men heaved the bushes overboard, and dug paddles frantically into the water. All night long, with the treacherous moon spotlighting them, they battled to keep ahead of the Riccarees.

On and on they swept, stopping for nothing that night or through the following day. And as they fled from the Indians he loved, Catlin reflected dismally on the future. If the white man had already turned the Riccarees into venomous enemies, what would he do to the Crows, Sioux, Blackfeet, and Mandans?

Their backbreaking flight from the Riccarees at Grand River speeded their arrival at the Teton River and Fort Pierre, in the heart of Sioux country.

William Laidlaw's cordial greeting contained a warning. The affair of Shon-ka, The Dog, still rankled the Sioux. Bitter and frustrated, they felt that if The Dog could not be found Catlin would make just as good a victim.

"They keep asking when you'll return," Laidlaw said. "A big party is camped now at the mouth of the Cabri, about eighty miles downstream. You may never get past them, Cat—better take some overland route."

If he left his boat, he must leave not only his paintings and collection, but his easel and canvas as well. Without his art materials, the twelve-hundred mile jaunt to St. Louis would be a waste.

"I'll stick to the boat," Catlin said, "and take my chances."

After a rest of only two days, the three hardy boatmen pushed off for St. Louis on August 16.

Their hearts beat faster as they neared the Cabri, but the encounter was unexpectedly mild. When he spotted

125

the Sioux tepees, Catlin steered the skiff along the opposite shore of the broad river. Not suspecting that one of the far-off bearded boatmen was the Medicine Painter, the Sioux extended a casual invitation by skipping a few rifle bullets across the river.

"Keep going!" Catlin said to Bogard and Ba'tiste. "But pull easy—as if we don't have a worry in the world."

The Sioux idly watched, until the skiff disappeared around a bend. Then all three men paddled with all their might until they had traveled miles downstream.

From there on the passage was delightful. They hunted and fished, and Catlin filled portfolios with paintings and sketches of tribes and scenery. At night as he slept on sandbars, beside the gush and gurgle of the river, he heard howling of distant wolves and the peaceful snoring of his boatmates. Only rarely did he cry, "Pull, boys, pull! A war party! For your lives pull, or we're done!"

When they paused to rest at Cantonment Leavenworth, Catlin learned that ten thousand Pawnees had perished from smallpox. Because of this tragedy, brought by the white traders and whiskey sellers, the Pawnees now looked coldly on the whites. In scenes of great suffering, many Pawnees had hastened inevitable death by leaping from cliffs or stabbing themselves in the heart.

Smallpox was more deadly than the white man's guns. Only five years later Catlin's beloved Mandans were almost completely exterminated by an epidemic that left about forty survivors. Catlin's great friend, Four Bears, wept as he watched his wives and children and friends die one by one. With his nation destroyed, and the corpses of his family surrounding him in his lodge, he drew his robes about him and deliberately starved himself to death.

The strange customs and culture of the Mandans perished, but thanks to Catlin's labors students of mankind can still visualize the lost life of "The People of the Pheasants."

One autumn morning the ragged and bearded trio paddled past the great steamers at St. Louis, and landed at a wharf. Bogard and Ba'tiste helped carry Catlin's paintings and collection to a hotel. When the artist returned to the boat a few hours later he found it had been stolen! For months the boat had been unmolested at the villages of redmen, where there were no laws. Here in civilization it had not lasted one day.

Who are the savages, and who the civilized? Catlin wondered.

Ba'tiste and Bogard fared little better than the skiff. Pent up from years in the mountains, Bogard erupted into a joyous spree. It ended with Bogard staring sadly through the bars of a jail, his pockets stripped of his perilously earned dollars.

Catlin's reunion with William Clark and Ben O'Fallon was much happier. His old friends were astonished at his achievement.

"Incredible," murmured the Red Headed Chief as he inspected row upon row of paintings. "Cat, you must have worked like a man possessed!"

He and O'Fallon toted up the figures on Catlin's amazing summer. In eighty-six days on the Upper Missouri, from Fort Pierre northward, he had traveled by steamboat and skiff an average of eighteen miles a day.

He had studied long ceremonies like the four-day Okeepa, gone on exhausting buffalo hunts, written the long letters now creating a stir in the New York papers, and—

Here Clark shook his head in wonder. "Why, you must have more than a hundred and thirty-five paintings! How could you possibly do such an immense labor in such a short time?"

Catlin smiled shyly. The governor didn't even know about the hundreds of rapid pencil and pen sketches, or the journals packed with notes. On certain inspired days he had painted as many as six canvases.

The right man had gone to the right place at the right time. Seeing the chance to make his dream come true, an energetic man had blazed into creativity.

"I just caught fire, I guess," said Catlin. "And now— more than ever—I'm convinced my project is worth a lifetime." A sudden smile lightened his gravity. "You know, I've never had so much fun in my life!"

But the same forces that endangered the free life of Indians were already at work to impede Catlin's grand design. Behind the closed doors of American Fur Company offices judgments were being passed on the artist. Smiling enemies prepared to thwart his crusade.

A cholera epidemic that made travel on crowded steamboats unwise delayed Catlin's return to Clara. It was a harsh blow. For months he had dreamed of reunion with her. With his great labor done he longed more than ever to search her dark eyes for the approval and love that were always forthcoming.

Moodily, he prowled about William Clark's office.

The wise old governor put the brooding artist to work. When Clark negotiated Indian treaties Catlin was there to sign them as a witness. He also produced several historic paintings.

The Black Hawk War had just ended. In a fierce struggle on the Upper Mississippi to retain his tribal lands, the great Sauk war chief had lost to such soldiers as Lieutenant Jefferson Davis and Abraham Lincoln. Now the chief, his sons, and leading warriors were imprisoned only ten miles away, at Jefferson Barracks.

Sight of the proud warriors shackled by chains to heavy cannon balls deeply disturbed Catlin.

"Black Hawk has done nothing of which an Indian ought to be ashamed," the old chief cried. "He has fought the battles of his country against the white man, who came year after year to cheat his people and take away their lands. The white men despise the Indians and drive them from their homes."

Catlin painted Black Hawk and other Sauk and Fox warriors, but said little about them. After Black Hawk's statement no comment was necessary.

As autumn turned icy, travel became safer. Catlin headed east, but his glad reunion with Clara in Pittsburgh was marred by a return of his lung inflammation. His exhausted body desperately needed rest.

Clara bustled cheerily about their room, making it bloom with potted plants and wall hangings of Indian curios. Her quiet presence made bearable a bed-bound month of hacking misery. Between coughs and fevers, George clasped her soft hand and talked of his plans for next spring.

"I'll go farther this time," he said, eyes shining with fever and expectation. "Steam up again to Fort Union, and then on up the Yellowstone River with the trappers, far into the Rockies! I'll see the Crows and Blackfeet in their home villages, and Shoshones, Cheyennes—"

But his bright hopes were dimmed by the warning of a friend from St. Louis. "Pierre Chouteau may like you, Cat," the visitor said, "but he sure doesn't like your articles in the New York papers! When you attack the fur trade for cheating and soaking Indians in whiskey, you also attack Chouteau."

Alarmed, the artist dashed off a tactful note to Chouteau. As soon as he could rise from his sick bed he boarded a steamer for St. Louis.

Pierre Chouteau's greeting was cordial. He expressed deep interest in Catlin's work, and chuckled forgivingly about the *Commercial Advertiser* letters.

"I want to go to Union again," Catlin said in relief; suddenly his worries seemed foolish. "Either on the *Yellowstone* or that new boat, the *Assiniboin*—"

Chouteau's face saddened. "But Laidlaw has sent warnings, mon ami. Zee affair of Shon-ka has made Sioux hate you. Zey swear to take your scalp!"

As Chouteau clucked sorrowfully, Catlin turned cold inside. Shon-ka had been killed in the Black Hills. The warring bands were reconciled, and Catlin was no longer in danger. Both men knew this, but Chouteau smoothly insisted he could not have Catlin's blood on his hands. He could not risk sending him upriver again.

What he could not risk, of course, was Catlin's presence on a steamboat loaded with a complete distillery meant for illegal use in Fort Union. Imagine a fanatic for the Indian, connected with a crusading New York newspaper, spotting *that!*

Although none of his pleas budged the suave Chouteau, Catlin stubbornly remained in St. Louis. He retouched Indian portraits, painted copies for O'Fallon and Clark, and hoped.

The last hope exploded with the news that the company was taking only two guests upriver, Prince Maximilian of Neuweid and his Swiss artist, Karl Bodmer.

"Room for a Swiss artist, but not for me!" raged Catlin to William Clark.

The old general peered at him shrewdly. "Back East there's a big job to do, Cat," he said. "Show your pictures. Show 'em what the Indians are really like!"

There was little choice. Catlin returned East, and in April of that year, 1833, exhibited over a hundred Indian paintings in Pittsburgh. Most of them were still unfinished, and Catlin squirmed at the first-night comments on their crudity. But old Putnam Catlin and Clara stood loyally and proudly at his side.

At Clara's urging, Catlin explained to the audience the background of his canvases. His simple and sincere talk on Indians made a deep impression. Shortly thereafter the *Pittsburgh Gazette,* although noting the unfinished condition of the paintings, printed a favorable report on the work.

"There's a lot of work ahead," Catlin said. "Once my paintings are completed, they'll speak for themselves. Remember old Peale's Museum, father? I have material enough to fill it twice over!"

Eager to work without distraction, he and Clara holed up for months in the Pearl Street House of Cincinnati. All summer Catlin filled in details and colors of his canvasses. At night, with Clara encouraging him, he labored by candlelight to expand his *Commercial Advertiser* letters into a book.

He worked with his usual speed. On July 20 he bought a hundred frames from Kimball, the frame maker. On September 23 he bought seventy-six more. Five days later he shipped two crates of paintings to Ben O'Fallon, whose purchase of forty-six paintings in the early 1830s greatly eased Catlin's financial burdens. These sales, added to fees for occasional portraits and copies of his Indian paintings, enabled Catlin to earn a modest living.

Soon he put on a display that won him acclaim in Cincinnati. Handsome in his new thirty-seven dollar frock coat and his fourteen dollar pants, he presided over an exhibit of a hundred and forty pictures. He now had an equal number in a semi-finished state.

Judge Hall, an authority on Indians and editor of the *Western Monthly Magazine,* hailed it as the most extraordinary and interesting collection he had ever seen, a most valuable addition to the history and arts of the country.

But the lure of wild country and wild people never fully left George. In early winter he and Clara steamed down the Ohio, southward bound because of his lung condition. When they reached the Mississippi, Catlin sighed bitterly. Up near the headwaters of the mighty river were tribes he still had not seen—and he was going the other way!

He spent the winter on the sunny Gulf of Mexico, in Pensacola, where his brother James managed a bank. Although the balmy climate benefited his chest, Catlin was restless. He wrote to Secretary of War Cass and others, trying to gain a new entry into the wilds. Meanwhile, he painted the few Seminoles and other tribes about. He fretted at his contact with these unhappy people, in the early stages of the long and bitter war aimed at driving them out of Florida.

Nor was he at ease talking of business and real estate with his brother's friends. "I shall hail the day with pleasure," he wrote in his journal, "when I can again reach the free land of the lawless savage; far more agreeable to my ear is the Indian yell and war whoop than the civilized groans and murmurs about 'deposits,' 'banks,' 'boundary questions,' etc; and I vanish from this country with the sincere hope that these tedious words may become obsolete before I return."

He should have written, "*if* I return."

Authorization had come from the Secretary of War. Catlin could join a perilous trek into the land of the wild and little-known Comanches! In the full bloom of their unspoiled primitive ways, these savage horsemen feared no one. They had already terrified the Mexicans who claimed their lands, the Yankees pioneering the Santa Fe Trail and most other Plains tribes.

Their ferocity seemed to chill everybody except George Catlin.

Comanches

11: Disaster with the Dragoons

IN EARLY spring of 1834 Catlin and his wife parted at Natchez, on the Mississippi.

"Don't worry, Clara," the artist said. He glanced at the caissons and field guns being hoisted aboard the steamer *Arkansas,* which would take him up the Arkansas River to the remote frontier outpost of Fort Gibson. "You'll be safe in Illinois, with our friends in Alton—"

His wife clung to him. "You know why I'm worried!" she cried. "You're going into an unknown land, into God knows what dangers!"

"Yes—but I'll be with the First Regiment of Mounted Dragoons," Catlin said cheerfully. "More than seven hundred fighting men. It will be a picnic. It's our first march into that country, so you can be sure the army won't let anything go wrong!"

134

His words were to haunt him later. After Clara kissed him, wept, and obediently left for Alton, Catlin met a young friend from St. Louis, Joe Chadwick. This merry young adventurer and a Lieutenant Seaton were also bound for Gibson. They filled him in on the mess at the fort. In spite of a generous salary of eight dollars a month for privates, recruitment was lagging. The first five companies still had no uniforms. Morale was lower than the Arkansas River—which was so low that the steamer could barely scrape upstream.

The entire operation was so sluggish that for two months after their arrival at the fort they waited for tardy orders to assemble and train. Soldiers grumbled uneasily as the cool marching days of spring yielded to wilting weather. As if the Comanches wouldn't make things hot enough!

The delay might endanger the dragoons, Catlin thought as he rode out one day to see a Choctaw lacrosse game, but for him it had been time well spent. His supplies were packed and ready—even when entitled to draw army provisions by order of the war secretary he always proudly insisted on paying his own way—and he had found the two essentials for a long march: a good horse and a good companion.

The good companion blithely hummed a tune as he rode beside him. Merry Joe Chadwick, always quick with a joke but cool and capable in a pinch, made the ideal friend.

And who could ask for a better horse than Charlie? Sold by an aging owner who feared to ride such a spirited horse, Charlie had responded beautifully to patient days of gentling. Catlin leaned forward and stroked the long black mane of the powerful cream-colored mustang. "Good old Charlie," he murmured, and Charlie tossed his head and nickered.

They passed settlements of displaced tribes from the East with hardly a look. Catlin had already painted these Cherokees, Creeks, Chickasaws, Seminoles, Delawares, and others, but as always his interest was in wilder native tribes.

Soon they rode through an Osage village of bark-and-reed lodges. Catlin greeted the Osages with a friendly wave. Tallest of all Indians, the Osages were usually over six feet high, and strongly built. Some of them towered a full seven feet, plus an extra foot of gaudy topknot. They made marvelous models and, best of all, they stubbornly rejected the way of the white man. They wore skins, not calico, and they shunned whiskey.

Their pace quickened, and Catlin took out his sketchbook, as they neared the broad plain where the Choctaw ball game was just beginning. Always a devoted fan, Catlin attended every ball game within twenty or thirty miles.

In this championship match, more than six hundred barefoot men swarmed over the field. Each carried two ball sticks, with a net at one end for catching and hurling the ball. They wore "manes" of horsehair on their shoulders, and arching "tails" of white horsehair or eagle feathers.

Throughout a long and thrilling day, the Choctaws struggled to toss the ball through the goalposts. The winning score of one hundred goals took six or seven hours to achieve. Tricks, kicks, yells, bloody noses, bruised shins, lumpy skulls—all abounded in this wild melee. "A mob in riot!" exclaimed Joe. "Go to it, boys! Hit 'em harder!"

After the long game the exhausted and battered players gathered together like old friends. Catlin slipped a full sketchbook into his pocket. "The Choctaws don't know it," he said to Joe, "but I'll make sure this game will never be forgotten."

"Sure," said Joe cheerfully. "But just remember, when the Comanches play games the goal is more likely to be a hundred fresh scalps!"

The temperature read 108 degrees in the shade.

Banners, horses, and men wilted that mid-June day when the Dragoons at last rode from the fort. They numbered only five hundred, far below authorized strength, but made an impressive display with their separate troops of blacks, whites, bays, and palominos.

At the head of a mile-long column snaking over green hills, rode General Henry Leavenworth and Colonel Henry Dodge. Beside them, loosely assigned to the headquarters unit, were Catlin and Joe Chadwick. To shield his sketchbook from the glaring sun, Catlin carried a broad cotton umbrella.

At first the land was fruitful and pleasant in spite of the heat. Catlin and Joe galloped where they saw fit, chattering, hunting, and gathering mineral specimens. On the ninth day even General Leavenworth joined in a pell-mell buffalo chase.

Catlin saw the general take a nasty spill. Moments

later the severely injured man fainted in his arms. The first of many misfortunes had struck the Dragoons.

Now the cruel heat took its toll on man and earth. The green land turned gray and tan. Scum lay so thick on shriveling ponds that a frog could hop across without wetting its feet. Men and horses sickened from the foul water.

At the camp on the False Washita, two hundred miles from Gibson, almost half the regiment came down with "bilious fever," and men died daily.

From this sweltering pesthole, Catlin penned another letter for the *Commercial Advertiser* in the general's tent, with "a dragoon fanning the General, while he breathes forty or fifty breaths a minute, and writhes under a burning fever."

Ordered by the dying general to push on with all troopers still able to ride, Colonel Dodge rode out with about two hundred and fifty troopers to find the Comanches. The Dragoons had been organized to awe the Indians with a show of power. With their puny force dwindling each day from fever, however, many began to dread meeting the warlike Comanches.

But they rode on. Distant smoke signals rising from hilltops and, daily, fresh tracks, told them that the Comanches knew of their presence.

At times only Catlin seemed eager to meet the Comanches.

"We're too weak to lick a band of schoolgirls," a trooper grumbled. "Comanches would massacre us!"

"If they do," said Joe Chadwick, "I'll bet George will have his easel set up, recording the whole thing!"

Joe cast a sharp look at the artist, who was mopping sweat from his pale face. "Cat! Are you coming down with fever?"

"And miss the chance to paint Comanches?" said Catlin. "Never!"

But his head ached, and his body burned.

Four days past the False Washita the leaders of the Dragoons drew up abruptly. A large party of horsemen was boldly outlined on a distant ridge. At last the Comanches were showing themselves. Their lances glittered and blazed in the sun.

Colonel Dodge looked at his thin line of ailing troopers, and gave orders to advance. A mile short of the Comanches he halted, and sent forward a man with a white flag. The Indians responded with a wildly riding horseman who bore a piece of white buffalo skin on the tip of his fourteen-foot lance.

Tacking back and forth with brilliant horsemanship, the Comanche made such a proud display of greeting the whites that Catlin later painted the scene. After much handshaking between white and red, a peace pipe was lit. The colonel gravely assured the Indians of the peaceful purpose of his expedition. Accepting this purpose with more faith than Catlin, the Comanches agreed to guide the Dragoons to their great village.

The trek over the baking Oklahoma plains cruelly taxed Catlin. Part of the time he was a litter case, but again and again he struggled to his feet and forced himself to sketch or paint. Joe vainly pleaded with him to rest. Eager to display their skill, the Comanches were putting on a show too good to miss.

"Finest riders in the world," marveled Catlin. A Comanche could shield himself from enemy weapons with the body of his horse. Dangling in a horizontal position to one side, with only a heel hooked over the horse's back, he could shoot arrows accurately from under his mount's neck. Some daredevils even shot arrows from under the horse's belly. They pursued buffalo recklessly, and once stampeded a herd smack into the regiment column, upsetting horses and dragoons.

Comanches lived by the horse. Herds of small, strong steeds, of many different colors, roamed these prairies. A lone Comanche with a rawhide lasso could catch and tame one of the fleet animals within a few hours. The taming was a tense and exhausting battle of muscle and will, which Catlin eagerly recorded.

The excitement drained his energy. Only pride and devotion to his cause kept his limp, aching body in the saddle for the grueling ride. Still, his eyes brightened when at last the party paused atop a ridge overlooking a valley near the Wichita Mountains. Below them stretched the Comanche village of six hundred tepees. Thousands of horses grazed near by.

The Comanche greeting was terrifying. Screeching like demons, hundreds of mounted warriors raced toward them. Dodge hastily prepared for the worst. The bugle sounded, and the feeble regiment drew up in three compact columns.

"It would take them just about ten minutes to wipe us out," Joe muttered to Catlin, as they braced for a battle.

Even the artist half expected an attack. If a war party, bristling with arms, trespassed into the heart of your

140

country, shouldn't they be treated as enemies? So it must seem to the Comanches, who were always ready to fight. Amazingly, Colonel Dodge's simple assertion that he had come as a friend had already worked its magic. The red-skinned horde suddenly formed into a line like well-disciplined cavalry. A white buffalo hide was planted beside the Dragoons' white flag—and it became apparent that the Indians were unarmed. The ferocious Comanches had galloped out to shake hands!

"You see, Joe," Catlin observed, as the relieved Dragoons rode into the swarming village. "Indians never let me down."

And Catlin never let the Indians down. Although shaken by "fever and ague," he labored daily under the searing sun to paint his record of Comanches and their ways.

His old umbrella caused a sensation. Knives, dogs, horses, squaws, and mules were offered in exchange for the strange object. Catlin refused all trades. In his ailing condition, he could not work unprotected from the fiery rays. He would not yield the umbrella for a herd of horses.

He shuffled on aching legs to observe ball games, and decided that Sioux were better ball players, but that Comanches were peerless horsemen. His hands shook as he painted a chief, The Mountain of Rock, who was so huge that he weighed over three hundred pounds. The artist privately called him "Mountain of Flesh." He liked the lean bodies of most Indians, and thought that obesity was an ugly and awkward affliction of civilized society.

Each day his chills became more violent. Bones began

to show under his sallow skin. Joe tried to help him, but no one knew exactly how to combat the sickness. Moaning, vomiting, shaking troopers were common; many had already been buried.

Under orders to counsel with the leaders of the Pawnee Picts or Wichitas who dwelt farther to the west on the edge of the Rockies, Colonel Dodge decided to complete the mission while some Dragoons still remained.

He looked closely at Catlin's haggard face. "I'm leaving litter cases here, with a guard to care for them," he said. "Can you still ride, Cat?"

"Clear to the Pacific, Colonel. Charlie can take me anywhere."

A pitiful little fortification of timber and brush breastworks was constructed to protect the sick men and their guards. It was a meaningless gesture; the whites were completely at the mercy of the Comanches.

On the morning of the departure for the Pawnee Picts Joe Chadwick cinched a saddle on Charlie, and led him to Catlin. The artist had clothed himself, but now lay helpless on his buffalo robe, burning with fever and too weak to stir.

Joe knelt at his side. "We've got to stay, Cat. Forget the Pawnee Picts."

Catlin grimly forced himself to sit up; he rose shakily to his knees, to his feet, took one step toward Charlie— and collapsed. Joe gently bathed his flaming face.

"Joe," whispered Catlin, "go. You go. Take notes. Make sketches."

As a good friend, Joe knew this was the best way to help the artist. He mounted his little buffalo chaser and rode off with the Dragoons, wondering whether he would ever see Catlin again.

In the following days, racked by an intermittent fever, Catlin occasionally revived enough to force his pencil over the sketchpad and to write in his journal.

"After an absence of fifteen days," he wrote, "the command returned in a fatigued and destitute condition with scarcely anything to eat, or chance of getting anything here. Colonel Dodge ordered a move to the head of the Canadian River, a distance of an hundred or more miles, where the Indians said there would be immense herds of buffaloes; a place to eat and restore the sick, who now occupy a great number of litters. Some days have elapsed, however, and we are not quite ready for the start. During that time parties of the Pawnee Picts, Wacos, and Kiowas have come up to get a look at us . . . I can scarcely be idle where so many subjects for my brush and my pen are gathering about me."

Joe Chadwick, who seemed immune to the fever, had made careful notes and sketches on his harrowing journey. He gladly donated them to Catlin's growing fund of Indian lore.

Somehow Catlin found strength enough to mount Charlie once more, for the cruel six-day journey to the Canadian River. The march was over high dry ground. Suffering from thirst was intense. Day after day they drooped along under a sun glaring from a cloudless sky. The grass had dried to tinder. The only water lay in stagnant pools, in which buffalo wallowed like hogs in mud. When the parched troopers drove the buffalo away, their horses plunged their noses into the pools, sucking

143

up the dirty and poisonous liquid so greedily that in some instances they fell dead in their tracks.

The men were almost as uncontrolled. Catlin and the others fell beside the muddy pools, drinking the warm and disgusting stuff even though they knew it caused their fatal fevers. The alternative was death by thirst.

At the Canadian River the Dragoons made a brief stop to rest and to hunt buffalo. It was a melancholy camp, with the officers' tents converted to hospitals that resounded with continual sighs and groans and moans. News of the death of General Leavenworth deepened the gloom.

After leaving the Canadian, Catlin weakened swiftly. Joe patiently hoisted him on and off Charlie each day, but one morning the artist was too feeble to sit upright. He was put into a baggage wagon with several sick soldiers. For eight days he lay in delirium on the hard planks, jarred and jolted until the worn skin of his elbows and legs was raw and bleeding.

When the living skeletons rode at last into Fort Gibson, a third of the officers and men were missing, buried back along the trail. From the government's viewpoint, Colonel Dodge had succeeded. A peaceful contact had been made with the Indians of the Southwest. But in terms of human misery, disease and death, the expedition of the Dragoons was a disaster.

Catlin lay near death in the post hospital. Every few hours muffled drums beat at the burying ground. From his bed beside the window he daily saw good friends being lowered into the ground. Memories of his brother Julius, who had once written glowing letters from this very post, flitted uneasily through his mind. He dreamed longingly of Clara, and her hopes of bearing him a child soon.

As weeks passed with only slight recovery, Catlin grew desperate. Although Joe tried to cheer him with jokes and songs, he ached to escape from this place of disease and death, and to return to Clara.

Dr. Wright shook his head gravely when Catlin announced that he planned to go home the shortest and cheapest way—a five-hundred-mile jaunt alone across the prairies to the Missouri.

"You're a civilian," he said. "I can't stop you, but I think you're crazy."

Most of the others agreed with the doctor, and Joe Chadwick worriedly said he would be unable to accompany Catlin.

"If I get out on the prairies away from this burial ground, I may get better," Catlin said. "If I stay here, I know I'll die."

Joe agreed to ship his paintings and luggage down the river later, to be forwarded to St. Louis. One morning in early September he brought up Charlie from his pasture. He saddled him, spread a bearskin and a buffalo robe on the saddle, and tied a coffeepot and tin cup to it. A half of a ham, a few pounds of hard biscuit, and some salt and coffee went into the food bag.

Joe helped his pale and shaky friend climb into the saddle. They clasped hands warmly. Then, with a wave at the head-shaking officers, Catlin rode off.

He carried a fowling piece in his hands, and pistols in his belt. On his back hung his sketchbook, in his pocket was a small compass to steer his way. And ahead lay five hundred miles of trackless country.

In the crisping autumn air, with Charlie prancing under him, Catlin felt a sudden surge of freedom and exhilaration. He galloped over green fields waving with wild flowers, away from the gloom and horror of the hospital.

With each hour he felt strength returning. Now and then he dismounted to lie in the grass for an hour or so, until the grim shaking of his chill and fever had run its course.

He was not lonely crossing the lonely land, for Charlie was an old and close friend. Catlin talked with him, argued with him, ate with him. At night they slept near each other, the artist on his bearskin, with the saddle for a pillow and the buffalo robe for a blanket. They slept in a great stillness broken only by the rustle of small night creatures in the grass, and the distant howling of wolves.

They lived off the land. While Charlie grazed, Catlin shot prairie hens, caught fish, and ate berries. With his health and optimism returning, Catlin cheerfully forded and swam streams, although the flood-swollen Osage River gave him some worries.

Spread far over its banks, the muddy torrent made a serious obstacle. Catlin stripped Charlie, and built a small raft to ferry his gear. Then he drove Charlie into the river, and anxiously watched until the sturdy horse reached the opposite bank. Next, stripped as completely as Charlie, Catlin shoved the raft into the river and pushed it before him through the angry swirling waters. The current

146

swept him half a mile downstream before he struggled ashore, to find Charlie waiting for him.

After twenty-five days on the prairie they reached Boonville, Missouri. Catlin crossed the Missouri River, and soon thereafter rejoined Clara at Alton.

News of the disasters had preceded him. Clara fell into his arms, weeping with relief. "Oh, how tragic it all was!" she cried.

Tragic in many ways, yes. But Catlin's trip was a great success, and he knew it. He had made the first paintings of wildlife and scenery in the Arkansas River Valley and of important Southern Plains tribes. He had made the first portraits of the shamefully displaced Creeks, Choctaws and Cherokees in their strange new land. The work was second in importance only to his great Upper Missouri series of 1832.

Breaking a Wild Horse

Crow, Ba-da-ah-chondu, He Who Outjumps All

12: An End. A Beginning

AFTER A winter in New Orleans and on the Gulf, the Catlins steamed thousands of miles up the Mississippi to Fort Snelling, a great pile of stone atop a bluff commanding the junction of the St. Peter's River (now the Minnesota) with the Mississippi.

Major Lawrence Taliaferro, the experienced and capable Indian agent at Fort Snelling, was eager to help. He arranged ball plays and dances, and acquainted Catlin with the Chippewas, who dominated land east of the river, and the Sioux, who controlled lands to the west.

Although it was a joy to have Clara at his side while he worked, now and then a pang of sadness struck the artist. He sensed that a beloved phase of his life was nearing an end.

148

"My job is only half complete when I finish painting the Indians in their primitive state," he said. "The other part is to get the world to see it all, to understand. That may be much harder."

Awareness of this task before him might have sharpened his usual pleasure in painting Indians—but it did not. It pleased him to see Chippewa women crowd around Clara to show their children, and to present their maple-sugar products to their gentle and sympathetic visitor. It interested him to see the woodland Chippewas (or Ojibways) cleverly use birchbark for lodges and light, graceful canoes. But it depressed him to see the decline of the half-civilized tribes about Fort Snelling.

The eastern Sioux, for instance, made a sorry contrast with their proud brethren of the Upper Missouri. Without beaver and buffalo, they were poorly clad and fed. Whiskey and disease sapped their bodies and morale.

Nevertheless, he painted them. "I'm interested in all Indians," he told Clara, "but it's only the primitive ones that *excite* me."

He painted, too, because he felt an obligation to round out his portrayal of Indian life. After Crows and Comanches, however, these ailing tribes were such a letdown that his adventurous spirit needed a lift. He decided to paddle one of the tricky Chippewa bark canoes nine hundred miles down the Mississippi to St. Louis, painting as he went.

Shortly after Clara boarded a steamer for Prairie du Chien, Catlin shoved off in his canoe with a Corporal Allen as a companion. About thirty miles below Fort Snelling a drunken brave ran out of a Sioux lodge, and blasted a charge of buckshot at them. It splashed water in their faces, and struck the canoe.

Catlin's temper flared. With a savage twist of the paddle he ran the canoe into shore.

"Watch it, sir," cried Allen. "There's a couple more, and they're all drunk."

Catlin nodded grimly, and reached for some bullets and his double-barreled gun. No man was more tolerant than he of occasional faults of Indians, but what excuse could there be for drunken shooting and possible murder? It had to be stopped. When bullets flew, a man must get tough—and George Catlin could be tough as rawhide when necessary.

As the Indians reeled forward, hooting and laughing, Catlin leaped ashore. "Keep me covered," he snapped to the corporal. Then, scowling menacingly, he advanced toward the Indians.

His stern face, and the two guns trained unwaveringly on them, cowed the Indians. They halted, fidgeting sullenly as Catlin angrily threatened to wipe out the lot of them.

Under the muzzle of his gun, he made hasty likenesses of them in his sketchbook, to send to Taliaferro, their feared and respected agent. Then, covered by the corporal, he withdrew, and they continued downstream.

After some miles, Catlin calmed down enough to explain to the shaken corporal: "For years they've been abused and made drunkards by white men. So when they get drunk, naturally they return insult for injury."

Perhaps the corporal wondered about a white man who could so easily excuse redskins. Although the trip was a sportsman's delight thereafter, the corporal abandoned ship at Prairie du Chien, only a few hundred miles from Snelling.

After comparing notes with Clara, Catlin followed alone in a canoe as she steamed to Dubuque, Iowa. When he caught up to Clara once again, they visited the Dubuque lead mines and Fort des Moines. Then Catlin went alone to visit Keokuk. After Black Hawk's disastrous war, sly old Keokuk had been made First Chief of the Sauks and Foxes.

Keokuk's vanity and fine appearance made him one of Catlin's best subjects. One full-length portrait in his best finery did not satisfy Keokuk. Aware of his splendid appearance on his beautiful black horse, he pranced and danced the animal before Catlin's door until the artist depicted the scene.

Catlin canoed toward St. Louis in a nostalgic mood. Changes seemed certain not only for Indians, but for himself as well. He paused for a half day to gather mineral specimens on the banks and to ponder his future. How much longer could he live his free adventurous life? He was thirty-nine now, rather late in the day for a man to start having the family which both he and Clara wanted.

He gazed pensively at the foaming rapids, and the distant hoot of a steamer bucking upstream brought him to a sudden decision. Why not hitch a ride back to Fort des Moines, where he could book passage for St. Louis? Eager to surprise Clara, he stored the minerals beside a pair of pistols and a fowling piece, and shoved out into the river.

In the distance downstream the steamer was picking its way up the channel. The artist's lean, hard muscles skilfully drove the canoe over choppy water toward the big boat. Viewers from the deck mistook him for an Indian because of his mastery of the tricky canoe. They waved to him as he drew near enough to hear the pounding of the steamer's engine and the hiss of its steam.

"Just one proper Indian twist of the paddle," Catlin said to himself, "and I'll pull right up to its side."

He gave the proper twist—but the current was swift and treacherous. Water boiled up from behind the paddle wheel. Suddenly the bow of his canoe rose skyward on the crest of a freakish wave. Balancing himself as if on a bucking horse, he coolly fought to keep the tipsy craft upright. At that moment a helpful but clumsy deckhand hurled a rope toward him. Catlin fell backward as the heavy rope struck his head.

In a split second the canoe capsized, and its contents, including the artist, were sinking toward the bottom of the Mississippi. A moment later Catlin bobbed to the surface, gasping and snorting. Strong hands hauled him aboard.

With his drenched buckskins clinging to him like another skin, he peered in dismay downstream. Minerals and weapons, of course, were gone forever—but what of the precious case crammed with notes of his travels? There it was, floating downstream beside the capsized canoe!

"Let me off!" he cried. Though warned he should wrap himself in blankets and relax, he insisted on being let off at the first point to pursue his cherished possessions.

Eventually, bedraggled and exhausted, he retrieved

case and canoe. Before a crackling fire he spread out his clothes, his papers and himself.

As the heat dried them all out, his frown of disgust slowly vanished. The warmth crept into his bones, and soon he was smiling. At last he laughed aloud. What a fool he must have looked, he thought, trying to out-shine the Indian with a paddle!

Back in St. Louis, he proudly introduced his pretty Clara to General Clark, and steered her through gay garden parties at Ben O'Fallon's. Best of all, Joe Chadwick turned up to have his portrait painted before leaving to join the Texan army.

Catlin's painting room rang with laughter as he exchanged stories with his kind and faithful partner of the Comanche campaign. Catlin told how he had capsized his canoe. Joe struck comic poses, and demanded that the artist make him look handsome.

But when Catlin returned East with Clara, some months later, he added a sad note to his journal. ". . . Joe was taken prisoner in the first battle that he fought, and was amongst the four hundred prisoners who were shot down in cold blood . . ."

That winter, 1835-36, Catlin worked hard on plans as well as paintings. Now and then he paused wearily to gaze out over the ice-covered Erie Canal, which ran past his studio in Utica, New York. The second part of his grand design must be fulfilled, and would be—but organizing an exhibit was turning out to be a harder task than expected.

Not until July, 1836, near his fortieth birthday, did he feel ready for a tryout. In a former Baptist church in Buffalo, New York, he displayed his paintings and thousands of Indian costumes, weapons and curios. Remembering Peale's Museum, he arranged the curios on racks and in cases along the walls under long rows of paintings. He stood with an easel at his side to hold the paintings on which he lectured.

Henceforth his income depended mainly on the sale of admission tickets to his show, not on the sale of paintings. Fortunately, the Buffalo press gave him good notices, and the curious public flocked in. To his surprise, many inquired about his collection of Indian pipes, with their ornately carved bowls of red stone.

"By gosh," a farmer would say, "I've plowed up a power of Injun pipes. Where do they come from? What are they *for?*"

Catlin explained that pipe-smoking was a solemn ritual in every phase of Indian peace or war. The bowls were made of a certain red claystone found in the fabled Pipestone Quarry. Tribes from all over the country obtained their stone from this sacred ground, on which no white man had ever been permitted to set foot.

"The location is rather vague," said Catlin. His pulse quickened with the sudden urge to seek out the quarry. "But it's somewhere in Sioux country, west of Fort Snelling."

Hunting the quarry made a grand excuse for another jaunt into the wilderness. Although the exhibit and lectures were a success, Catlin gratefully fled the hall and steamed over the Great Lakes to Green Bay, in Wisconsin territory. At ease once more, he painted canoe races, Menominies, Winnebagoes and Chippewas netting immense quantities of white fish.

Robert Wood, a wealthy young English adventurer eager to dare the taboo of the Quarry, joined him at Green Bay. Five husky French voyageurs sped them up the winding Fox River in a huge bark passenger canoe. Wood strummed a guitar, and voyageurs sang lustily as the canoe slid past prairies and acres of wild rice on the way to Fort Winnebago.

Lighthearted in spite of constant warnings, Wood and Catlin then paddled in a small canoe down the Wisconsin and then up the Mississippi and the St. Peter's to LeBlanc's trading post.

The trader repeated the familiar warning. "The Sioux guard the holy ground for all Indians. Whites have tried to enter. They were killed!"

"Probably they were rascals out to exploit the Indians," said Catlin. "If we approach with respect and good will—"

"Bah!" LeBlanc's swarthy face contorted in disgust. "There's a party of mean braves prowling hereabouts, spoiling for trouble—"

He broke off, open-mouthed, staring over Catlin's shoulder. The artist turned. A tall, hawk-faced Sioux warrior had slipped quietly into the cabin. In came another, and then another—more and more until they almost filled the tiny room. LeBlanc backed against the wall, close to his rifle. Catlin and Wood stood their ground, their calm faces belying their racing hearts.

A flashing-eyed warrior spoke. "You are sent to see

what the quarry is worth. If whites can't buy it, they will get it some other way!"

"How! How!" the Indians chorused. One by one they stepped forward to speak:

"I speak strong, my heart is strong. The red stone was given to the red men by the Great Spirit. It is part of their flesh. If white men took some away a hole would be made, and blood would never stop running!"

"We know the whites are like a great cloud that rises in the east, and will cover the whole country. We know they will steal all our lands—but if they ever steal our quarry they will pay dear for it!"

Hour after hour the angry Indians spoke and threatened. Temperature and tension rose dangerously in the stuffy room. Beads of sweat glistened on LeBlanc's face. His eyes rolled gratefully when his husky son entered. Catlin and Wood listened politely, nodding now and then in agreement.

At last Catlin was permitted to reply. Showing some sample paintings, he explained his background and long friendship for the Indians. The fame of the White Medicine Painter had spread through the west, and a few of the warriors seemed impressed.

But the tall warrior advanced angrily, shaking his fist. "No white man has ever been to the quarry. No white man shall ever go to it. You have heard what I have to say. You must go back."

He seemed about to assault the unflinching artist. Young LeBlanc leaped forward, and with one blow knocked the Indian to the floor.

Catlin tensed. The hands of the warriors dropped to

their knives and tomahawks. They crouched forward, breathing fast, their eyes cold and hateful. LeBlanc wrenched his rifle from the wall. All poised for action. The tiniest spark could ignite a deadly explosion.

A vision of Clara flashed through Catlin's mind. Soon she would bear him a child. But unless he quelled the fires of hate raging about him he would never live to see that child.

He raised his hand in the sign of peace. "I come in peace," he said. He bent forward, and helped the groggy Sioux to his feet. "I have nothing but love in my heart for the Indian, and I think that the Indian is wise. He may not know how to make rifles and steamboats, but he is very wise."

It was hard to be eloquent, dependent on his smattering of Sioux, sign language, and an occasional phrase from LeBlanc, but he must try. His voice crooned and gentled, as if he were dealing with a panicky horse. The red men stared at him unblinkingly as if they had been carved from pipestone, but they listened.

"Because he is wise," Catlin continued, "he knows the white men are too many and too strong and they will take the country. It is bad, and I grieve for it, but the Indian is wise and he knows this. But there are good white men and bad white men. The bad ones will try to take the quarry and make themselves rich."

He paused, then his voice rang loud and strong. "I will go to the quarry. I will do as much as any red man to keep white men from stealing it. But I must see it to describe it so that whites will understand this holy ground and honor it, and keep it for the Indians."

He stopped. Had he convinced them? Their faces were impassive, but surely they must understand that he wanted to help.

Only the brave with the swollen jaw spoke. "I have spoken," he said, still angry. He whirled and stalked out the door. The others silently followed.

"Go back, for God's sake!" cried LeBlanc. "Go back, or they may scalp me, too."

Catlin looked at Wood, who winked back at him reassuringly. Like Joe Chadwick, the fearless Englishman took everything as a lark.

"We'll go on," said Catlin, and the trader shrugged despairingly. He outfitted them with horses, and waved farewell as if they would never return.

"I'm ready for anything," Wood said, "but my hunch is you won the whole battle right there in the cabin. They listened, Cat—and they knew you were right!"

The lovely grassy swells seemed too peaceful to harbor any menace. Catlin smiled faintly, and said, "We'll see."

After a while Wood began to play his guitar and sing lighthearted songs. Since Catlin could not carry a tune, he contributed to the entertainment by spinning yarns about Indians. They had always justified his faith in them, he concluded, so he and Wood might as well relax and enjoy the trip.

Occasionally Wood turned serious. "You must take your paintings to Europe some day, Cat," he said. "They'd create a sensation."

"That's what Murray said." Last year the Catlins had met the Honorable Charles Murray, a young British

158

aristocrat who had explored the plains and become fond of Indians.

"Murray can pull the right strings," said Wood. "He's a son of the Earl of Dunmore, a nephew of the Duke of Hamilton. Have him arrange a show, Cat!"

Catlin laughed. "Let's get home safely first!"

Beneath their chatter both were alert for any sudden war whoop. But Catlin's appeal to wisdom and good will had worked. It was almost an anti-climax when a half-breed trader, La Framboise, guided them without incident straight to the great quarry.

Situated in the rising country of present Pipestone County, Minnesota, the famed quarry fascinated Catlin. Before a cliff twenty-five feet high and nearly two miles long were the diggings where Indians for centuries had obtained the soft red stone.

Years ago Catlin had mused about geology with his brother Julius. With Joe Chadwick he had gathered stones and fossilized sea shells from the arid plains of Oklahoma. Now, as he hefted a piece of soft red stone, his mind churned once again with the mysteries of the earth. Why had this quartzite cliff before him risen out of the prairie grass? What had formed the quarry? How could you explain the presence of five great boulders of gneiss, felspar and mica, hundreds of miles from their logical source? What caused the earth's crust to rise and fall?

He sighed, and loaded more stone into his pockets. The answers were locked in stone. Maybe some day he would find time to search for them.

Meanwhile, as Wood twanged his guitar in the

distance, the artist set up his easel. As he painted a panoramic view of the quarry, a feeling of kinship grew within him for the tribes who had come here over the ages. He almost felt the presence of their Great Spirit who had here made the first pipe.

This is a holy place, he thought. A place of myth and magic. May it always be respected.

On his return home, Catlin sent samples of the stone to Dr. Charles Jackson of Boston, a leading mineralogist. Jackson termed it a new mineral compound, and gave it the name which it bears today, Catlinite.

It was a fitting honor to mark the end of Catlin's great work on the prairies—and to herald the birth of his daughter, Elizabeth. But there was little time for celebration, for now Catlin resolutely turned his back to the open spaces that he loved, and plunged into combat with the civilization that he distrusted.

Sioux and Ojibway Pipes

Osceola, The Black Drink,
a Famous Seminole

13: The First Wild West Show

ON A frosty evening in late 1837, Catlin strode nervously toward Stuyvesant Institute on Broadway, in New York City. Clara, almost trotting to keep at his side, exclaimed at the great crowds milling in the street.

"Why, George! They're trying to get in your Indian Gallery. You're a success. A *big* success!"

Catlin smiled wryly, recalling the labors of the past year: the retouching of hundreds of paintings; the framing and crating; the disappointing tryouts in Albany, and then Troy; his recurrent illnesses; the tedious haggling over contracts; the printing of posters, and publicity sessions; the hateful hours of poring over account books—

No more tramping over the prairies to visit fascinating

new Indian tribes. No time for canoeing, hunting, fishing, or gazing at the wild landscapes he loved.

No time for anything but work.

No time even for Clara, and his lovely new daughter Elizabeth. In his spare moments he kissed them, fondled them, chatted with them—but business left few spare moments. Ten thousand details nagged at him, tore him from his family.

Fortunately, New Yorkers were eager to pay fifty cents to see his vast collection of 494 paintings, covering 48 tribes.

Money poured in. Crowded out of Clinton Hall by the eager mobs, Catlin rented the larger Stuyvesant Institute. This was the public's first chance to see what the fabled West was really like, and he offered a bountiful look. Apart from paintings numerous enough to cram a large museum, there was a huge collection of bows and arrows, quivers, musical instruments, weapons, pipes, a towering Crow lodge, mineral specimens, and countless other items.

Catlin hoped that this vast Indian Gallery would form the nucleus of a National Museum in Washington, D. C., to be sponsored and financed by the government. Without conceit, he knew that he had created a national treasure which should belong to the nation as a whole.

Such a museum would best serve his original purpose: to preserve the appearance and customs of the doomed primitive Indians. However, it might well help the surviving Indians, too. As a constant reminder to the Washington legislators of their responsibility, the grave red faces would work for justice. But Catlin knew that working for the Indian would be an uphill battle.

"Have you seen how disappointed some of the audience are?" he asked Clara. Every night, while his Irish assistant, Daniel Kavanaugh, placed one painting after another on a floodlit easel, Catlin talked about each painting and the warrior depicted. "They want blood and savagery, not truth. They want to hear that Indians do nothing but torture children and massacre white men. What nonsense! When they hear the truth, they don't believe it."

"They do, George," Clara said soothingly. "You're so sincere, I'm sure they believe."

Catlin shook his head. "It isn't only the ignorant laymen," he brooded. "They perk up at the Mandan torture scenes, of course—and that's just where the know-it-all scholars sniff and turn up their noses! As if I'd invented it for cheap sensationalism!"

"Hush!" said Clara. "People wll think you're angry at *me!*"

A quick smile softened his stern face; he squeezed her arm affectionately, and said, "Let's go in, dear, and try once more to convince a house full of skeptics. This mob turned up because Keokuk and some of his tribe agreed to attend my talk. Fifteen hundred customers—at the special price of a dollar apiece!"

Before the crowded audience Catlin took the offensive. He displayed his painting of Keokuk on his beautiful war horse, and said: "Many have scoffed about this horse. They say no frontier Indian ever rode so fine a creature."

He gestured at Keokuk, but he and his warriors had already leaped up and started to jabber at sight of the picture. Touchy and proud, Keokuk spoke angrily when the interpreter explained the charge. "Why can't Keokuk ride as good a horse as any white man? That is Keokuk's horse! If he had not been a fine horse, Keokuk would not have bought him!"

The room rocked with applause. The interpreter added that he too recognized the horse—for he had sold it to Keokuk for three hundred dollars.

Catlin pursued his advantage by firing a series of questions at the Indians on points which had aroused doubts in the East. The Indians backed him on every point.

Catlin's friend and publisher, Colonel William Stone, took the floor and moved that the meeting vote complete belief in the truth of Catlin's paintings and statements. Again the hall thundered with applause. Choking with emotion, Catlin expressed his thanks.

The newspaper stories of his triumph attracted large audiences. More important to Catlin, many intellectuals and scientists now swung over to his side. At forty-one, he had won both prestige and prosperity. America's first Wild West show was proving the appeal, which endures to this day, of the wide open spaces.

But in December of 1837 a tragic event caused Catlin to shut down his show overnight, and to leave New York for Fort Moultrie in South Carolina.

Osceola, The Black Drink, The Tiger of the Everglades, had been treacherously captured.

For six years Osceola had led his Florida Seminoles so skilfully that they had eluded and outfought the best troops of the U. S. Army. Unable to capture him otherwise, the army had violated all principles of honor. When Osceola had come forth with four of his aides and two hundred warriors to confer with General Jessup—under a flag of truce—the army had seized him and bundled his manacled men off to prison.

Seething with rage, Catlin hurried to Fort Moultrie. While there he painted an outstanding portrait of the great Seminole leader. The painting was the basis for later lithographs which became famous collector's items.

Osceola fell ill from his chronic malaria. Suspicious for good reason of white men, he refused the care of the post surgeon, and accepted only an Indian doctor. The night of January 27 he was so ill that Catlin and some sympathetic officers sat up with him all night. When he rallied, Catlin left to catch his steamer for New York. The next day Osceola died.

After his death, the post surgeon cut off Osceola's head and took it home. Whenever he wanted to punish his two small sons, he hung the Indian's head on their bedstead.

Osceola's betrayal and death put new fire into Catlin's lectures, new force into his plans to storm Washington, D. C. His hardheaded and prospering brother-in-law, Dudley Gregory, tried to stop him from moving his show to the capital.

"You'll lose your shirt," he said. "Think of the moving expense alone, George! Your stuff will fill a boxcar. And what for?"

"I'm gaining support in New York for the Indian cause," Catlin said. "But it's the support of the federal government that I need."

"Bah! What if some congressmen *do* see your show? How many votes do Indians have? None! How much do they contribute to the party? Not a dime!"

"I've been hoping for some news—" said Catlin, breaking off as Clara entered holding a letter. Elizabeth, clinging to her mother's skirt, toddled beside her. The artist excused himself, ripped open the letter—and smiled triumphantly.

"Great news!" he cried. He picked up Elizabeth, and tossed her high over his head. She screamed with laughter. "If only you could read, my sweet little papoose!" he said. "The House of Representatives has passed a resolution to consider buying my Gallery!"

Clara joyfully flung her arms about them. As the family happily embraced, Dudley Gregory scanned the letter, and dourly shook his head. "It will die without a peep," he said. "The Senate has to approve—and they won't."

The elated family tried to calm down and listen respectfully to Gregory's warnings.

"Face the facts of life, George," said Gregory, brandishing his cigar. "Washington, D. C. is a southern town, mostly—and the south wants to push Indians out of their lands to make way for more slave states. You'll never overcome that opposition."

"I'll try."

For Clara's sake, Gregory tried to conceal his irritation. "Why be pigheaded?" he demanded. "Putting on this show and touring it is a tremendous job and not one you're cut out for. It's a businessman's job, coping with a million petty details. It's a circus-man's job, dragging in customers off the streets. But it's certainly *not* an artist's job! It's killing you, George. That's why you're always ailing lately."

Catlin brushed aside the objections.

"Then what of your family?" cried the brother-in-law, his face reddening. "Give Clara a good secure home, instead of a series of cheap hotels and boarding houses. You've got a child now, and another on the way. It's time to settle down!"

"Clara understands," Catlin said softly. He looked at his wife, and she nodded proudly.

"Indeed I do. You're a great man, George. The world must see your work."

Catlin looked gravely at his tiny daughter. "And what do you say, Elizabeth?"

"Da," she said. "Da-da."

"See?" said the artist to his fuming brother-in-law. "It's unanimous."

Gregory hurled his cigar into the fireplace. Desperately, he made one last try.

"Crusading for those ignorant Indians," he said, "will wreck your finances, harm your health, damage your family—and *ruin you as an artist!*" Catlin winced. Clara's face whitened. "You can't go politicking and crusading and cluttering up your mind and draining energies with your exhibit, and still paint! Oh, you may toss off a copy now and then, but that isn't being an artist. Art is a full-time job. If you stick to your easel, study your craft, and take up portraits again, you'll be a great artist, George. Go on this way—and you'll kill the artist."

167

Catlin hesitated. There was much truth in Gregory's appeal.

"If that's the price I must pay," he said at last, "I'll pay."

In the spring of 1838 Catlin opened his exhibit in Washington, D. C. His fertile mind had hatched a new theme for his lectures: a National Park, a broad strip of Western prairie to be kept forever unspoiled and intact, with its native tribes and herds of buffalo. Here for ages to come the world would see the Indian, with bow and lance, in feather and deerskin, pursuing the buffalo and elk. Man, beast, and land alike would be saved in all their wildness and beauty.

Thus Catlin was the first American to call for what later evolved into our National Park system. Such an idea was much too advanced for Congress, but the artist's determined eloquence won him powerful friends. Daniel Webster and Henry Clay strongly supported the National Museum idea, and campaigned for the purchase of the Indian Gallery.

Final decisions, however, were nowhere in sight when falling receipts forced Catlin to leave the capital. Money for the heavy expenses of the show and of his growing family came from ticket sales, so Catlin moved on to tap new audiences in Baltimore, Philadelphia, and Boston.

Through letters and frequent trips to Washington, Catlin lobbied for the purchase of his collection, but the government moved with the speed of a glacier. He decided to shock it into action.

His friend Murray was now connected with Queen

Victoria's court, and had invited Catlin to bring his show to London, assuring him it would be a great success.

"Appeals to sentiment and to the love of art and science don't budge Congress," Catlin observed to his wife. "But if I sting their patriotism, they may hop!"

The artist tossed his bombshell: he would take his entire collection to Europe, and possibly sell it to a foreign government.

When his exhibit reopened in New York in 1839 Catlin boldly pursued his bluff—for bluff it was. He had no great desire to go to England; his supreme ambition was to see his collection in a United States National Museum. But in newspaper ads and from his speaking platform he repeated his intention of going to Europe.

Newspapers reacted with a storm of editorials bewailing the decision, and urging Congress to keep Catlin's priceless Americana where it belonged, in America.

Catlin waited for an offer—but no offer came.

Laid low for six weeks at this crucial time, by a serious hip injury, Catlin fired letter after letter to Washington begging for action. At the same time, to make his bluff look convincing, he made complete plans to go to England with his exhibit.

And still Congress dawdled.

By the autumn of 1839 Catlin realized he had been caught in his own trap. Only one course remained: he must make good on his published statements by taking his collection abroad.

He held a gloomy conference with Clara and his aging father. A widower now, Putnam Catlin had deeply enjoyed his recent stay with his artist son, but he nodded firmly at the decision.

"Go abroad, son," he quavered, well aware that once he returned to his Pennsylvania farm he would probably not live to see George again. "Think of it as a new phase of an old crusade. You'll win, if you endure."

But Clara's eyes filled with tears. Expecting her second child, she must defer any overseas trip to a later date.

"I moved heaven and earth, but I can't move Congress," Catlin said. "I promised them to cancel the trip at the very last moment. I promised to return from Europe at a week's notice, and not to sell abroad for twice whatever Congress offers," He sighed, and stroked the silky hair of his daughter Elizabeth. "Promises, promises. And they're all mine. In spite of Webster's orations, nothing happens."

"Suppose some foreign government does try to buy the collection," said Clara, bravely trying to cheer up her depressed husband. "Congress will act in a hurry then!"

"Yes indeed!" cried Catlin. His eyes flashed. He rose, and began to pace, faster and faster. "We ought to see Europe anyway, Clara. And it's certainly time that Europe saw what our wild America really is!"

Clara and Putnam Catlin smiled at each other as Catlin's optimism revived—as it always did. In a moment the artist was speculating on the great things to come. But Clara's smile hid a gnawing fear: this new adventure might bring disappointment and tragedy.

Choctaw Champion Ball Player

14: Indians on the Thames

ON NOVEMBER 25, 1839, at the age of forty-three, Catlin sailed on the packet boat *Roscius* for England. With him as aides were his towering nephew, Theodore Burr Catlin, and Daniel Kavanaugh, a cheerful, talkative Irishman. His eight tons of freight included six hundred paintings and several thousand Indian costumes, weapons, and curios.

Shortly after landing, Catlin rented three large gallery rooms in Egyptian Hall, Piccadilly, London, at almost three thousand dollars a year. Charles Murray came to see the paintings being hung in the big main gallery, over a hundred feet long and with the latest in gas-lighting fixtures.

"Capital!" exclaimed Murray. "By Jove, you've worked—and so have I. I'm trying to get the social and intellectual elite to turn out for your show. A good start makes all the difference, y'know."

"That's why I've invited fifty-one newspaper editors," said Catlin. He was determined that this great gamble, involving all his money and much of his reputation, must not fail. "I may not be a born showman, but I've learned. Publicity is all-important."

Their joint efforts brought in a horde of lords, baronets, knights, dukes and duchesses, bishops, earls and countesses for the preview—as well as many literary and scientific authorities and editors. The novel and exciting show delighted them all.

In short order the newspapers and fashionable salons buzzed with talk of Catlin's Indian Gallery. Such favorable comment guaranteed a smash hit. Londoners jammed the public opening on February 1, 1840, eager to pay a shilling apiece to see the latest sensation. They kept Catlin busy from morning until night answering questions, even though his formal lectures came in the evenings.

The success was gratifying, but exhausting. One night Catlin slumped into a chair after his show and glanced wearily at the latest newspaper clippings about his show.

"Ah," said Daniel brightly, "isn't it a grand thing to be a celebrity!"

Catlin nudged a stack of envelopes on his desk. "Invitations to tea, to dinner, to a hundred fine homes. Very grand, Daniel—but when does a celebrity get time to rest?"

Dark shadows ringed his eyes; his face was gaunt and fatigued. The strain of constant lecturing and socializing, and the gloom of lonely nights in hotel rooms, were sapping his strength.

"Well now, the doctor said cut down the social folderol and spend half time at the gallery," said Daniel. "As to questions, faith, by now I'm knowing all the answers—and if I don't, a bit of Blarney will provide 'em!"

Catlin turned over a part of his duties to Daniel, politely refused many social invitations—and then worked harder than ever. His pen, already busy on happy letters to his wife about the birth of their second daughter, Clara Gregory Catlin, now scratched incessantly to complete a long-contemplated book. A greatly expanded version of his popular letters from the prairies to the *Commercial Advirtiser,* it bore a title almost as long as its author's journeys: *Letters and Notes on the Manners, Customs, and Condition of the North American Indians.*

When London publishers shied away from the expense of printing two thick volumes with 312 steel engravings derived from Catlin's paintings, the artist was crushed—but only temporarily. Boldly, he decided to publish it himself at his own expense.

The book came out in October, 1841. It had many flaws. It sprawled, disorderly and imprecise. Its events were confusingly out of sequence, and were sugared with high-faluting tributes to the glories of Nature. Its crude engravings did not do justice to Catlin's skill.

But it was an instant critical success, for good reason.

Letters and Notes combined the thrills of an adventure tale with more solid facts on Indian life of the plains than had ever before been available. Catlin's fervor sparkled through all its faults, and made them trivial. His crusading love for the Indian and his indignation at injustice gave the book life, and touched it here and there with passion. An exciting and authentic new world opened up for its readers. The most popular and influential of all Catlin's books, it has since gone through countless editions.

An avalanche of praise descended from England's foremost newspapers and literary periodicals. Young Burr Catlin clipped the reviews and saved them.

"Wait till Aunt Clara sees this!" he cried, holding up fifteen pages of praise from the famous *Edinburgh Review*.

" 'Mr. Catlin is one of the most remarkable men of the age,' " quoted Daniel. "It must be so, for 'tis here in black and white."

"The book is making me famous," admitted Catlin wryly. "But at what price? It cost a small fortune to publish—and it's not selling!"

"At twelve dollars a copy, how could it?" said Daniel. "That's more than many earn in a month! Lower the price and you'll sell more surely—and then lose more, too, on each copy you sell! Ah, I fear you must take the credit, sir, and let the cash go!"

Catlin resumed nightly talks at Egyptian Hall to make up for the financial loss on his book. The increased activity left him pale and drawn. As he breathed the foul and foggy air of London he longed for his clean open spaces, and found solace only in the arrival on the *British Queen* of Clara and his two daughters.

He happily whisked them off to a snug little home known as Rose Cottage in suburban Waltham Green. And at last the Catlins sampled, for a while, the simple joys of home life.

As befit a famous father, Catlin rashly hired an English nursemaid and an Irish cook to staff Rose Cottage. "I've got everything but money," he said ruefully to Clara. "If your brother could see my account books, how he'd shake his head! The Gallery expenses are—"

"Tush!" said Clara. She linked her arm in his, and smiled at her daughters playing in the garden outside. "We're together at last. That's what counts."

"How true, how true!" exclaimed Catlin. "But if only the Congress would make up their minds!"

Suddenly Clara was tugging him through the door. "It's time you played at being a father, George!" she said. "Come to the garden—and learn how to hold your daughters on your knees!"

Knee-dandling was pleasant, but a nursemaid and a cook and pretty dresses for his three pretty ladies cost money. As attendance declined with the waning novelty of his Gallery, Catlin lured new audiences with Tableaux Vivants—actors painted and dressed in Indian costumes, painstakingly coached to dance and sing like true redskins. So that they could authentically enact battles, ball games and ceremonies, the artist assumed the role of choreographer and stage director.

"I know it isn't art," Catlin admitted to Clara, "but it attracts the public. Remember Peale's Museum. The public has to be excited!"

175

Clara was too happy to protest. There were many joys and a few sorrows in those years. When Catlin wasn't too busy they led a gay social life. They took honors at a gala masquerade ball by appearing in authentic costumes. Catlin even met Queen Victoria, and showed her his model of Niagara Falls.

But no word came from the United States about purchasing the collection. The inaction gnawed inside Catlin like an ulcer. "Some day," "soon," "inevitably," his friends wrote about the purchase—but nothing happened.

In 1842 Catlin grieved over the death of his father. This is my consolation, he thought as he embraced his family and tuned his good ear to the sweet gurgle and coo of his third daughter, named Victoria in honor of the Queen.

Meanwhile, as years passed, audiences inevitably declined at Egyptian Hall. The only remedy, Catlin told his wife, was to tour the show through Britain. That would raise enough money for a return to America in comfort.

Much as she loved Rose Cottage, Clara was eager to depart. "Let's go home soon," she said. "Then you can concentrate once more on being an artist—the great artist that you should be."

Cheerful at the prospect of returning home, Catlin took his troupe on a six-month tour of Manchester, Edinburgh, Dublin, and many other cities and towns. With twenty men on his hands, and all their expenses and problems to burden him, he needed all his optimism and energy. Near the end of his tour, in Liverpool, he gladly announced it was his last showing before his departure for New York.

Clara was already packing the family garments when the plans to return home were shattered by what seemed a stroke of good fortune. A man named Arthur Rankin turned up with nine Canadian Ojibway Indians, and suggested that they join Catlin's show.

Rankin was a cheap speculator, and Catlin had always opposed bringing Indians abroad on speculation. Now that they were already here, however, Catlin saw both an obligation and an opportunity.

"Rankin has put the Ojibways in an awkward spot," he told his disappointed wife. "If I don't help they'll be completely stranded. Besides, think what a sensation real Indians will make!"

"Very well." Clara meekly opened a suitcase and began to unpack. "But it's such a frightful drain on your health and time. When will you be able to paint?"

When indeed? Sometimes he longed to escape into his studio and do nothing but paint. Suppose he abandoned the Indian cause, as his brother-in-law had suggested, and concentrated solely on painting? He would become a fine artist, perhaps a great artist. He would see more of his family, make more money, and avoid the thousand headaches of showmanship; in short, he would be a most sensible man.

However, he had long since faced this issue squarely and made his decision: to him painting was not an end in itself, as it was to most artists. Instead it was merely a means to advance the cause of Indians, and to acquaint the world with a people he loved and admired.

177

Why brood, then, about idle easels and wasting brushes while Ojibways languished, helpless and dependent in a strange land?

"It won't be long, dear," Catlin assured her. "I long to go home as much as you do."

As Catlin expected, the Ojibways made such a dramatic appearance, with their onstage dancing, cavorting, and screeching, that excited audiences packed Egyptian Hall night after night. Rankin split a clear profit with Catlin of four hundred dollars a night—and immediately began to ache to keep it all. His ache intensified when Queen Victoria summoned Catlin and the Ojibways to Buckingham Palace for a command appearance.

Warmed by such good fortune, Catlin could not suspect that a tide of bad luck was rolling in toward him. One early hint of misfortune lay in the scoffing attitude of some of the press which once had praised his paintings. They termed the Indian performances a cheap and shabby sideshow. Worse still, Arthur Rankin treacherously betrayed Catlin in an incident involving Cadotte, an English-speaking Ojibway who had fallen in love with a pretty little London girl.

"We'll have to discourage Cadotte," Catlin said worriedly to Rankin. "Their marriage would be doomed. I've seen happy marriages between white and red—but not between Piccadilly and the prairies. He'd never stay in this smoky city and she certainly wouldn't settle down as a squaw scraping buffalo skins in his tepee!"

"Too late," said Rankin smoothly. "I've already given Cadotte permission to marry her."

"But you can't!" cried Catlin.

178

"Ah, but I can," said Rankin, in a deliberate taunt. "According to our deal, you handle only the exhibitions. Outside the hall the Indians are my charges, not yours."

Catlin stood up so swiftly that he almost upset the table before him. "I refuse to sanction this," he said curtly. "It's a tragic mistake for both of them."

"In that case," Rankin said, "consider our partnership broken. You're not indispensable, Catlin. I've heard your line of gab often enough to repeat it—and I will!"

Outraged, Catlin stalked from the room, just as Rankin had planned. Shortly thereafter Rankin opened with the Indians in a room directly adjoining Catlin's gallery. Posing as one who had spent his life among Indians, he announced he would lecture. Poor Catlin was left at the very start of the season with a big hall for which he had signed an expensive lease—a hall which he could not possibly fill without a live attraction.

Rankin tried to publicize his show by making a spectacle of Cadotte's marriage. Bands blared forth from the tops of the flower-decked four-horse coaches that paraded the wedding party through the main streets of London to the church. Before the ceremony Rankin announced that the bride would henceforth appear on the platform with the Indians, playing the piano.

The unscrupulous promoter had gone too far. England's proper Victorians rose in wrath at such commercialization of the sacrament of marriage. When Rankin opened the show he had stolen he was almost hooted off the stage. Although Catlin was blameless in the affair, some of the mud stuck to him.

The attendance at Egyptian Hall, with only his paint-

179

ings and collection on view, was so meager that Catlin let Daniel run it completely, at a loss, while he labored on his next work. This was the *North American Indian Portfolio,* a beautiful series of colored lithographs. Issued in 1844, it was snapped up by collectors such as the Emperor of Russia and the King of the Belgians.

Another beautiful new issue was Catlin's son, George Catlin, Jr. The infant was a constant joy to his father. He was cooing in Catlin's lap the day the artist spoke to Clara about a new move.

"My work is done here," he said. "I've taught England whatever I can about Indians. Perhaps I've done some good. I've certainly done well for my reputation. But I've been too long from my living models." He swooped the baby through the air, laughing. "Soon as this fellow is big enough, we'll sail for America!"

Instead of the expected smile of joy, a frown pinched Clara's face. "What's wrong?" he asked.

She gestured nervously at the black headlines of a newspaper. "Still another shipwreck. There have been so many lately!" Her effort to smile failed. "Oh, I know it's foolish to worry, but with all the children—"

She sighed, and was silent.

George Catlin was always a man of action. True, shipwrecks *were* dangerous. Why not do something about it?

Catlin's answer was an ingenious invention. Its purpose was to save lives at sea in times of disaster, by disengaging and floating the quarterdecks of steamers and other vessels. Catlin threw himself wholeheartedly into developing this device. After spending a great deal of

180

money and time, however, he learned that a similar invention had been patented some years before.

Undaunted, Catlin one day cheerfully brought home an old American acquaintance to meet Clara. She liked the straightforward and honest Mr. G. H. Melody on sight. A few minutes later she must have wished she had never seen him.

"Imagine, Clara," said Catlin excitedly, "the Secretary of War has permitted Mr. Melody to bring fourteen Iowa Indians here!"

Mr. Melody's project, in fact, was a rough forerunner of present-day cultural exchanges. The hope was that these carefully selected Indians would benefit through contact with European life, and bring back some of its benefits to their primitive tribes. In those days, though, neither the cultural nor the financial problems of such missions had yet been solved.

"We need help," said Mr. Melody. "How can we make a living in England?"

Clara blanched, but kept silent while her husband carefully allowed he'd like to see the Iowas first.

One look at the Iowas exploded Catlin's doubts. These famous warriors made the Ojibways look pallid and over-civilized. Three of them, White Cloud, Walking Rain and Fast Dancer, he had painted on the prairies.

"Chip-pe-ho-la!" they shouted their Indian name for him, and seized his hand. "Chip-pe-ho-la!"

Almost before he knew it, Catlin embarked on a new partnership with Melody and arranged for a show in Egyptian Hall. But summer was a poor time for exhibitions; furthermore, the bad odor of the Rankin episode still lingered. Even though the Iowas were so wild and impressive that notables like the great statesman, Benjamin Disraeli, invited the party to lunch, business was sluggish.

Catlin's small savings dwindled rapidly. Hoping that a tour to new cities through the British Isles would be profitable, he once again left Egyptian Hall. But now the slow tide of misfortune was running stronger. The damp smoky climate sickened several Iowas. The infant son of Little Wolf died of pneumonia in his father's arms, and Roman Nose died of consumption in a Liverpool hospital.

With the zest and good cheer of the Iowas decreasing, Melody and Catlin strove to make their trip worthwhile. Almost daily they took the Indians to museums, churches, and places of interest. To the Iowas civilization seemed even stranger than the Mandan village had once seemed to Catlin.

By now Catlin hewed so closely to the Indian viewpoint that he often shared their reactions to the sights.

They listened to white men preach temperance—and counted hundreds of taverns in every large city.

They listened to white men preach charity—and then saw beggars in the streets, and men thrown in jail for not being able to pay their debts.

They puzzled over fox hunts, for who would eat fox steaks?

They visited the appalling coal mines at Newcastle, where horses and mules lived in perpetual darkness. Here blackened women and children, with coal carts strapped to their waists, crept on their hands and knees to draw the burden through places too small for horses. In darkness lit only by a small candle they crept through mud and water, while their legs bled from cuts.

They saw better things, too. Catlin enthusiastically pointed out the lofty cathedrals, the hospitals, the bustling industry, the signs of wealth and power. But he never forgot the coal mines. What Indian torture equalled this?

England and Englishmen were admirable—but oh, for a fresh prairie breeze to clear the fog and smoke from his lungs! Oh, for a view of rolling plains, big sky, buffalo and simple redskins—the only subjects that would ever excite his brush!

Meanwhile, dust thickened on his palette, as he struggled with crushing problems. For the survival of all—his family, his collection, the Indians—he simply must draw in paying customers.

His lectures became more and more hair-raising as he stretched truth into fiction in a desperate effort to thrill the public. Dignified Englishmen who had once vied to play host to the great artist and ethnologist now ignored the sideshow barker.

Clara cringed at the slow descent, under pressure, from idealist, artist and crusader into blatant showman. When Catlin announced that he must go to Paris, to recoup his fortunes with the Iowas, she begged him not to.

"You're abusing your genius, George. You belong at your easel—not at the head of a three-ring circus." Tears brimmed from her lovely dark eyes. After years of patient acceptance, at last she demanded something of her husband. "I want to go home!" she cried. "Give the Indians to Melody—do anything with them. But take us home!"

Catlin tenderly enfolded her in his arms. "I will, Clara," he said soothingly. "I swear. But first won't you come to Paris with me? The children would love to see it—and so would we! And I've already promised the Iowas." He tilted her face toward his. She smiled through her tears. "After a few months we'll all sail from France for home."

She nodded, happy because she knew that Catlin would keep his pledge to return her to America. And so he would—but not at all in the way he had intended.

Sioux Women Dressing Hides

Mandan Archer

15: Triumphs and Tragedies

APRIL OF 1845 found the Catlin family settled in a comfortable Paris apartment overlooking the Church of the Madeleine. Artful by now at publicity, George held a meeting with Burr and Daniel.

"Now, lads," he said, "the French bureaucrats will fuss through their red tape for weeks, maybe months, before approving our show. Let's use that time to tantalize all of Paris!"

His strategy, after a barrage of posters and ads, was to tease Parisians with brief glimpses of the Iowas, and let curiosity and rumor take over. Much of the time the Iowas remained concealed in their rooms at the Hotel Victoria. Wide-eyed chambermaids, refusing to go near

185

them, whispered that the savages had cannibal teeth. Their dark hints at other mysteries set people speculating about the strange red men who had discarded their beds and slept on floors.

The curious craned their necks for a peek at the Indians when Catlin took them on carriage rides across Paris, but the carriage curtains were drawn. Now and then, though, came an exciting glimpse of feathers, glittering eyes, or a hawklike profile, when one of the Iowas parted the curtains to satisfy his own curiosity.

People began to ache for a good look at the Iowas. Catlin triumphantly capped the publicity buildup by gaining an audience for his Indians before King Louis Philippe in the famous Palace of the Tuileries. Under the gilded ceilings that had looked down on the pomp of the brilliant royal courts, the Iowas danced, warwhooped, and brandished tomahawks until the glittering chandeliers swung.

With the poise that had come from facing the rulers of America and Britain, Catlin explained Indian ways to the Queen and the royal guests. Louis Philippe already knew a good deal about Indians.

Smiling into his whiskers at the memory of his youth, the monarch said, "I, too, have visited the American wilderness. *Oui,* I slept in the wigwams of Oneidas, and Shawnees, and Cherokees. I paddled a skiff down the Ohio and the Mississippi rivers to New Orleans!"

"Vive le roi!" shouted the Indians. Catlin had rehearsed them for a week. *"Vive le roi!"*

With this amiable encounter, the Indians became the talk of Paris.

When the exhibit and lectures opened on June 3, 1845, crowds flocked into the spacious Salle Valentino. Wild whooping and the twang of bowstrings on an archery range fifty yards long gave zest to this original Wild West Show, which took place the year before Buffalo Bill Cody was born.

All kinds of celebrities turned out to see this new sensation. Ambassadors, the prefect of police, noted artists, leading editors and famous writers eagerly sought the honor of strolling arm in arm with the handsome buckskinned painter past his long row of paintings. Catlin met as an equal Victor Hugo, the great poet and author of *Les Miserables,* and enchanted him with tales of the prairies. Accustomed by now to startling sights, Catlin barely lifted an eyebrow on meeting the woman novelist George Sand, who wore trousers and puffed on a cigar.

When he brought the Iowas to the Louvre for a private tour at the invitation of the director of that great museum, he found the most distinguished man of all waiting for him.

An elderly man with a pink complexion and lively blue eyes firmly grasped his hand. "Delighted to meet you," he said cordially. It was Baron Alexander von Humboldt, regarded by Catlin and many others as the most famous man of the century. Anthropologist, astronomer, botanist, explorer, geologist, geographer, geophysicist, meteorologist, oceanographer, writer and zoologist, Humboldt was practically the godfather of modern science.

Catlin beamed with pleasure at meeting this man who

187

had mastered so many sciences at which the artist, although interested, could only dabble.

"You can teach me much about Indians, Herr Catlin," modestly said the man who had explored much of North and South America.

"You, sir, can teach me much about everything!"

They strolled together through room after room of the Louvre, chuckling at the astonishment of the Iowas, who until this moment had thought that Catlin's collection of paintings was surely the largest in the world. The hours flew as they discussed art, science, and Indians.

A few days later Humboldt called at the Salle Valentino for a private view of Catlin's exhibition. His emphatic approval of the paintings, as well as his interest in Catlin's theories on geology and the origin of Indians, left the artist in a happy glow.

Meanwhile the Iowas were rapidly becoming homesick. As the novelty of civilization waned, they longed for their own villages and prairies. Ill omens troubled The Doctor, who now awoke nightly with nightmares.

Suddenly Little Wolf's wife died. The Iowas met in solemn council. Many of them were coughing from lung afflictions picked up in England. All of them were gloomy. First a little child, then a warrior, and now a squaw had died.

Was this misfortune Catlin's fault? Some claimed it was. The Doctor and Chief White Cloud agreed that Catlin was blameless—almost. He worked hard to help the Indians still on the prairies and the Indians yet to be born. However, his work was bad for the Indians in Paris.

They summoned Mr. Melody and gave their decision. "They will stay six nights longer in Paris, Cat," said Melody later. "And then they must go home."

Catlin was pacing up and down, his brow wrinkled with worry. "It's for the best," he muttered. "They should be in America." He wrung his hands, and gazed in anguish at the closed bedroom door. "How I wish we all were there! I'm like the Indians, Melody. Away from prairies and forest and rivers my strength slowly drains away." Again he glanced worriedly at the door. "Maybe Clara is the same way."

"She'll be all right," Melody said uncomfortably. "It's only a cold."

In July, 1845, Melody sailed from Havre for New York with the Iowas, who had learned one great thing from their educational trip: "There's no place like home."

Catlin hardly noted their departure. Clara's cold had developed into pneumonia. He hovered constantly at her bedside, gently restraining her when she tried to rise in her delirium. In quieter moments, she recalled happy moments of the past.

"Remember the picnics with Julius? Dear Julius . . . And the lovely garden at Rose Cottage? . . . Your father was so proud at your first exhibition, almost as proud as I was . . ." She raised herself on her elbows. "Oh, George, take me home! Please!"

He soothed her tenderly, and cursed himself for having brought her to Europe against her own real desires.

On July 28 Clara Catlin died, two months short of her thirty-eighth birthday.

Numb with shock, Catlin kept his promise to send

her home. In December of 1845 Clara was buried in the Gregory plot of Greenwood Cemetery, Brooklyn, New York.

With four motherless children to tend, the grief-stricken father fought to rise above his own despair and sense of guilt. As the bewildered children clustered about him for his warm outpourings of affection, he noted with a pang the resemblance to Clara of Elizabeth, his eldest daughter. Tenderly, he touched her cheek; tenderly, he shepherded them into slow acceptance of the cruelty of death.

At the same time, he needed more money than ever to support the children properly. A party of Ojibways arrived, pleading for Catlin to take over their exhibition, which had failed in England. To fill the gap left by the departed Iowas, Catlin installed them in the Salle Valentino.

Daniel shook his head gloomily each night as he toted up the receipts for the new show. "The toast of Paris one month, and just stale bread the next! What's happened to the crowds?"

"Some idiots are spreading rumors that our Indians are only dressed-up Frenchmen," said Burr indignantly.

"Never mind," said Catlin. "Our luck is changing. King Louis Philippe has invited me to breakfast, to meet the King and Queen of Belgium! And he wants a private show of my collection in the Louvre! We're not out of fashion yet!"

But the luck was only partly good. Louis Philippe commissioned Catlin to paint fifteen copies of his Indian paintings. However, with the collection tied up in the

Louvre, no exhibit was possible in the huge and expensive Salle Valentino. Meanwhile, the idle and hungry Ojibways ran up large bills for room and board, charged to Catlin.

Seeking funds to return them to England, at least, Catlin took the Ojibway troupe to Belgium. The children were left in the care of their nurse. "Daddy will be back soon," Catlin assured them. "Then we'll be closer than ever."

Interest in the show ran so high in Belgium that a profitable run seemed certain, but just before the opening tragedy struck once again. The Ojibways came down with smallpox. A few days later one was dead, and six were in a Brussels hospital, at Catlin's expense.

"We can't let the poor fellows down," Catlin told Daniel, but the good-natured Irishman made a sour face.

"Aye. But you mustn't be letting yourself down either! There's little enough money to start with!"

"They're alone and in a strange country," Catlin said stubbornly. "When I was alone and sick in *their* country, they fed me and warmed me and an Indian offered me his body as a pillow."

Daniel shrugged, and was quiet. When it came to Indians, he felt, there was no reasoning with Catlin.

Although Catlin obtained the best care, two more Indians died. A full two months later, after much care and worry, Catlin was free to return to Paris. He had not earned a cent for himself, of course, but his unceasing efforts had raised funds to ship the survivors back to America.

"Most of the funds," growled Daniel, "are after

coming from your own pockets—almost eighteen hundred dollars! Faith, when will we ever see that much again?"

It was January of 1846. Now Catlin settled down to finish his commission for the king. He put his collection in storage and, to be closer to the childern, turned one room of the spacious apartment into a painting studio. The ache in his heart for Clara was eased by the nearness of his youngsters.

As he neared fifty, painting came harder to him, perhaps because he had neglected it so long, but he was always glad to be interrupted by little George. Proudly beating his drums, the child often toddled into his studio.

He was so persistent with his drums, or tambours, that Catlin said, "The Tambour Major, that's what I'll call you, Georgie."

George rattled his drums, and strutted past the easel. The three daughters giggled. Aged ten, eight, and six now, they loved the afternoons of window-shopping on the boulevards with their father, and the evenings of adventurous yarns about the West.

Meanwhile, the cause that never left his mind for long once again absorbed him. He launched a new campaign of letter writing to induce the government to purchase his Indian Gallery, offering it to Congress for sixty-five thousand dollars.

"I've got to get action, Burr," he told his nephew, who was still on his payroll at over two dollars per day. "Funds are so low I may be forced to sell to one of those English noblemen who seem so interested."

Help for his cause came from eleven prominent Ameri-

192

can painters in Paris. Shocked that an artist honored by official commissions from France should be ignored by his own country, they petitioned Congress to buy the entire collection.

At last Congress stirred. A committee found Catlin's price most reasonable, and urged that the purchase be made. At the same time, another project dear to Catlin finally materialized. A bill was passed to establish the Smithsonian Institution.

Catlin chuckled at the news. "It took an Englishman, James Smithson, to provide the funds," he said, "but at last we're getting a National Museum—with a gallery of art just right for my collection!"

But Catlin's long series of misfortune and tragedy persisted. Suddenly the Mexican War broke out. While cannon boomed, all bills concerning art collections were tossed into congressional wastebaskets.

Catlin's reaction was to pick up his brush and start painting. With four children to support, he could not afford the luxury of mooning and moaning.

The completed series pleased King Louis Philippe. "Sit down, M'sieur Catlin," he said. "Let us talk about Indians and the great Mississippi."

They reminisced together. Catlin left with a royal commission: twenty-seven paintings to depict the four-year journey of the great explorer La Salle from the Great Lakes to the mouth of the Mississippi.

"It will tie me down to Paris," Catlin told Daniel, "but once I collect the three thousand dollars I'll be able to take the children back to America."

Before settling down to this long-range task, Catlin

made a quick trip to London in the late summer of 1846 to try to raise some money. While there he met Henry Rowe Schoolcraft, who had come from the United States mainly to see Catlin.

Catlin greeted Schoolcraft warmly, for in many ways he was a man after Catlin's own heart. Years before Schoolcraft had been an Indian Agent for Wisconsin Territory and the tribes near Lake Superior. Before that, as an explorer and traveler, he had discovered the source of the Mississippi at Lake Itasca. He devoted most of his life to the study of Indians, and wrote a great deal.

"I have an important task," he told Catlin. "I'm trying to get Congress to back an immense encyclopedia on the Indian tribes of America."

"Good idea," said Catlin. "Will the government really pay for it?"

"Of course. I'm certain I can get them to subsidize the whole thing!"

"More power to you," said Catlin ruefully. "I paid for my book out of my own pocket."

"You're just not a good politician, Catlin," Schoolcraft said, with just a touch of condescension. He was well aware of his own powers as a fluent and convincing speaker. "I'll have 'em eating out of my hands! Now—" He leaned forward with his most persuasive smile. "Naturally I plan to use your paintings as illustrations."

Catlin's eyes flashed. As an individualist, a loner who had labored mightily to create his collection, he had no intention of sharing it with an interloper. Furthermore, although Schoolcraft was an expert on the forest Indians near Lake Superior, he knew little of the Indians of the prairies and the Rockies.

Would this man be favored by Congress, and permitted to work for years on the government payroll, when Catlin himself could not even sell at a low price his priceless collection?

The irony of it rankled, and made Catlin speak with unusual curtness. "Sorry," he said, "it's absolutely out of the question. You cannot have my paintings."

Schoolcraft's smile faded. His face flushed. "Is that final, Mr. Catlin?" he said in a voice choked with anger.

"It is."

Schoolcraft stomped to the door. "Perhaps it's just as well," he said bitterly. "Why should I work with a common sideshow barker?"

He slammed the door as he left.

Catlin's rejection aroused a deep and lasting anger in this ambitious man. Back in the United States, Schoolcraft obtained another artist, Seth Eastman. While motions on Catlin's magnificent collection stalled, this slick politician pushed through Congressional approval of his own project. Then, with the comfort and security of a government subsidy, he settled back for years to produce six immense and dull volumes entitled *Historical and Statistical Information Respecting the History, Condition, and Prospects of the Indian Tribes of the United States.*

Henceforth, Schoolcraft never missed a chance to belittle Catlin and to sabotage his reputation.

Unaware he had made one of his few enemies, Catlin

returned to Paris. The rat-a-tat-tat of the little Tambour Major's drums and the gentle graces of his three daughters helped him forget his financial worries.

And suddenly financial worries seemed trivial. An epidemic of typhoid fever broke out in Paris. One by one the girls sickened and lay tossing and moaning. George, aged four, was sickest of all. Catlin kept a night-and-day vigil at the bedsides of his suffering children.

The girls recovered, but the little drum major died. As he set aside the battered drums, Catlin wept. His greatest joy and greatest hope for the future had departed.

"These few words flow in tears from the broken and burning heart of a fond father," Catlin wrote in his journal. "They take but a line or two, and are the only monument that will be raised to the memory of my dear little George, who lived, in the sweetness of his innocence, to gladden and then to break the heart of his doating parent; the only one while he was living to appreciate his loveliness; and now the only one to mourn for him."

Force of habit kept the heartbroken artist at his easel, but for the first time doubts of his powers assailed him. He was fifty now, and growing deafer. Once he could have tossed off the twenty-seven paintings due the king, but now they came slowly. The La Salle paintings, based on painstaking research and lively imagination, were bright with color, swirling with action—and yet strangely unconvincing. They lacked the reality of his Indian paintings.

Those who glimpsed the paintings as Catlin labored month after month on the four thousand human figures involved, whispered that Catlin was a second-rate artist.

The only good thing about any of his paintings, they said, was his exact reporting of novel subject matter.

"*Oui,* he is an intrepid traveler, but as a fine artist— pouf!"

Vastly more important were the opinions of a young man who had haunted the Salle Valentino and studied Catlin's portraits of Iowas in the annual Salon exhibit of Paris artists. Still in his mid-twenties, Pierre-Charles Baudelaire was not yet fully recognized as the great poet, art critic and talent-finder of his era. Apparently Catlin never even saw Baudelaire's private brochure of praise for his works.

Baudelaire delighted in the transparency and lightness of Catlin landscapes, especially, with their masterful use of Indian reds and prairie greens. But he praised the portraits, too, finding in them increased understanding of ancient sculpture.

The eyes of a poet looked beyond the occasional crudities and errors of draftsmanship, which are still criticized, and saw in the paintings a reflection of Catlin's own nature: a natural charm, simply expressed.

It was not a passing fancy of the great critic. Ten years later he fondly recalled Catlin's Indians, and in 1859 he scorned the French landscapes at the Salon as being vastly inferior to Catlin's.

High praise indeed, from the top critic of the art capital of the world. One sentence alone from Baudelaire, in which Catlin was linked with giants of the art world such as Veronese and Delacroix, guaranteed him a measure of renown.

Awareness of such appreciation might have sweetened

Catlin's bitter sorrows, but apparently even this consolation was denied him. In this dark period nothing went right for the artist.

In his full year of labor on the paintings for the king he ignored the political chaos sweeping Europe in the winter of 1847–48. His dulling ears barely heard the chants of discontented mobs in the Place Madeleine, outside his window: *"Vive le Reforme! Vive le Reforme!"*

He returned lighthearted from delivering the La Salle series to the Louvre. "Cheer up, kittens," he told his little girls. "In a few days we'll go shopping for pretty things—and not just window shopping either!"

Three days later the Paris mobs erupted into the revolution of 1848. The king and queen fled from the country. Soldiers of the Second Republic broke into Catlin's apartment. While the terrified girls cowered within the artist's protecting arms, the soldiers searched, as if for traitors.

"Friend of the king!" the soldiers cried at Catlin. "Friend of the fat pig! *This* for his friends—" And they ripped bayonets through half a dozen paintings.

The children wept, and finally the soldiers retreated, muttering threats. At fifty-two, Catlin could still be a man of action. He quickly organized a successful escape to England of his three girls and the entire Indian Gallery.

Of the three thousand dollars due him for a year's labor, however, he never collected a cent.

Hard pressed for money, he reopened the Indian Gallery at his new living quarters, 6, Waterloo Place, Pall Mall, London. Unfortunately, the fickle public and the wealthy collectors had lost interest.

"Customers are scarcer than dinosaur eggs," wailed Daniel. "Maybe they're extinct!"

Catlin smiled grimly. They were living on borrowed money now. "I may have to mortgage the collection, Daniel. I'm still painting copies to sell, but the prices are sinking as fast as we are."

Somehow he provided a governess, tutors, and dancing school for his daughters, but the girls saw little of him. Crushed by past tragedies and present burdens, he berated himself as a parent. His dainty girls needed genteel company, but what was he? A hunter, a fisherman, an expert with a canoe paddle, a man at home with Stone Age Indians and mountain men so crude that they tore the liver from the still-smoking carcass of a fresh-killed buffalo and ate it raw.

He spent his days in the gallery. At suppertime he met his daughters, for polite but increasingly remote conversations. Then he hurried to his writing desk. He wrote swiftly, rarely pausing to alter a word, on and on into the nights.

Eight Years' Travel and Residence In Europe was an attempt to show the reactions of Catlin's Indian troupes to civilization, and to restore Catlin's fame and fortune. The book was published late in 1848. Hastily and carelessly written at a time of emotional depression, it failed in all respects.

The critics who had hailed Catlin's first book scorned the second, and used the occasion to berate him as a cheap showman, a windy liar, a profiteer on Indians.

"The only hope now is Congress," Daniel muttered sadly to Burr, as they watched Catlin stoically accept the humiliation. "And a sorry hope it is. Will they *ever* be acting?"

As months and years passed, it seemed that Congress had forgotten its own recommendations to buy Catlin's collection. Catlin scrimped out a bare living through the occasional sale of a book or some drawings. Now and then interest in him revived briefly, as when he proposed a floating museum of primitive arts. He lectured nightly to small audiences. But the days of glory when he had met as an equal men like Baron Alexander von Humboldt, the famous explorer and geographer, seemed gone forever.

The financial decline continued. In 1851 Catlin uncomplainingly undertook to paint fifty-five copies of his original paintings for a British lord, at a pitiful rate of ten dollars apiece.

That same year he did a series of a hundred and sixty-seven beautiful pencil drawings, *Souvenirs of the North American Indians,* owned today by the New York Public Library. A year later he drew two more *Souvenirs,* as well as some smaller watercolor copies assembled as an *Album Unique.* No misfortune, it seemed, could permanently still his energetic interest in Indians.

"Great news!" cried Catlin, as he burst into his gallery. "Daniel, my lad, at last it's happened! The House of Representatives has voted to buy my collection for fifty thousand dollars!"

"The Lord be praised!" Daniel whooped, slapped his thigh—and then suddenly looked cautious. "But now it's up to the Senate. They must approve—"

"They will, they will," said Catlin confidently. "Webster himself is calling the collection more important than all the other drawings and representations on the face of the earth!"

With prospects so bright money lenders willingly advanced still more money to Catlin, who by now had mortgaged his collection and rashly speculated in the vain hope of solving his money problems. He blithely arranged for passage to Washington.

"We're going back to America," he cheerfully told his daughters. "In triumph!"

Back in the states, however, Henry Schoolcraft still nursed his resentment against Catlin. He worked actively against the purchase bill. More powerful forces also opposed it.

The Senate was evenly divided on the issue when Senator Jefferson Davis of Kentucky rose to speak. Davis recalled the Dragoons' expedition into Comanche country in 1834, when as a young lieutenant he had watched Catlin paint some of the pictures now under consideration.

Jefferson Davis admired Catlin's paintings; he knew they were authentic and he praised their value. Astonishingly, however, he ended his speech by saying that "on principle" he must vote *against* the purchase!

The southern slaveowners Jefferson Davis represented were hungry for Indian lands, and wanted no sympathy aroused for redskins. When the final vote was taken, Catlin's bill lost by one vote. Jefferson Davis, friend and admirer, had cast the deciding vote against Catlin.

News of the defeat struck Catlin's little world like an

earthquake. His creditors immediately closed in for the kill, like wolves with a stricken buffalo. The quickest and most vigorous of them was Joseph Harrison. The tough, wealthy American headed the largest locomotive factory in the world, the Harrison Boiler Works in Philadelphia, and had just built a railroad for the Russian czar. With a shower of dollar bills, Harrison paid off the major debts against the Indian Gallery. He swooped the collection out of England on the first ship bound for Philadelphia. There his men stored the crates in the basement of the Boiler Works.

Tardy creditors appeared, and angrily stripped the Catlin apartment of all furnishings, while the bewildered girls watched.

Back in America, the Gregory in-laws had long expected such a smashup. Dudley Gregory appeared on the scene, more prosperous than ever. The multimillionaire looked scornfully at his artist brother-in-law—at this queer, haggard man who had failed so miserably.

Gregory could have paid off Catlin's debts and retrieved the collection—indeed, he could even have built a museum without flinching at the expense. But why waste money on a hopeless case?

"I'm taking Clara's children," he said coldly. "They'll have a decent, comfortable home. The best of education. Everything money can buy."

What could Catlin do? At fifty-six his youth was gone. He had lost his wife and son, his money and his reputation, the collection that was his life's work, and now he was losing his daughters.

Standing bent and defeated in his naked gallery, he

nodded acceptance. He felt as desolate as the Ponca ancient he had seen on the prairie so many years ago, exposed and left to die.

The girls sailed away to comfort and wealth. Daniel and Burr returned to America. What happened to Catlin, nobody knows; later his memory was dim about those days of shock and misery.

Somehow he eluded his creditors with a few drawings and sketches, and returned to a cheap room in Paris. He shivered through the miserable winter of 1852–53, a suspicious figure on the boulevards with his hollow face and shabby greatcoat.

Too poor to heat his tiny room, he haunted the reading room of the Bibliotheque Imperial. In the company of other poverty-stricken intellectuals and researchers, he studied the South American *Travels* of his friend, Baron von Humboldt. Another scholar also was reading about South America, in old Spanish volumes.

"Fantastically rich gold mines!" the old man whispered to Catlin. "Fabulous. Abandoned to the savages in the Crystal Mountains of Brazil in wartime—and then forgotten. Think of the treasures waiting for some lucky man!"

The scholar glowed at the prospect—and then sighed. He was well aware he was not the type to chase a will-o'-the-wisp to South America.

George Catlin was made of sterner stuff. He studied the maps and volumes, and life flickered again in his slowly healing spirit. An ordinary man aged fifty-six, deaf and destitute, scorned by a world that once had honored him, might shrivel quietly into oblivion. But not George Catlin.

"Gold," he mused. "Gold and Indians. South America is full of Indians. I wonder—could I paint another collection?"

His eyes hazed over with dreams of a land where primitive people dwelt. Primitives, who had always treated him kindly, and knew nothing of money.

He thumped his fist so hard that books and eyebrows rose all along the reading table.

"I'm going to South America!" he cried to the astonished scholar. "I'm going to the Crystal Mountains!"

The scholar stared at him as if he were mad.

Minataree Sudatory—Steam Bath

Flatheads Fishing

16: The Fabulous Wanderer

THE STREETS of Georgetown, British Guiana, baked in humid, tropic heat. Dogs sprawled in the shade, barely stirring to snap their tormenting fleas. The perspiring young Englishman mopped his brow, and stared in surprise at the crowd in the street.

"I say, who'd put on a show in this steaming weather?" he said, and pushed forward. He found the crowd had gathered at the curious sight of the coppery heads of some Carib Indians looking out of a window.

"Some old duck is painting the ruddy savages," he heard. "Don't know where he found them."

The Englishman went inside, and paused in surprise at the sight of George Catlin. Bronzed by the equatorial sun, the artist brushed in the finishing touches on the portrait of an Indian chief.

Years ago the young man had met the artist in Egyptian Hall. Shyly he wondered whether the aging artist would recall him. At that moment Catlin put aside his brush and looked up. His blue eyes sparkled at the sight of the newcomer.

"Smythe!" he exclaimed, and strode forward with outstretched hand. "Good to see you."

In a moment Catlin was introducing Smythe to another sunburned gentleman, Dr. Hentz, a German botanist. Eager to show his work, he toured Smythe quickly about the room, which was lined with paintings of South American Indians and landscapes.

Although deafness had almost silenced his world, Catlin still talked with charm and vivacity in response to written or shouted questions.

"Landed in Caracas, Venezuela," he said briskly, bringing Smythe up-to-date on his travels. "No luggage but a few Indian portraits, some Bristol drawing board and art materials, a few maps and Humboldt's *Travels*. A brown derby on my head, and one of Colonel Colt's new revolving carbines in my hand!"

He gestured at a painting of three lovely Indian girls. Their bodies were whitened with clay for their modest and graceful dance on carpets of jaguar skin. "Sheer poetry, isn't it?" said Catlin. "And a great honor. The Glad Dance, or The Handsome Dance, hadn't been seen for years in Venezuela, they say. But they put it on for me!"

Smythe marveled at the artist's vivacity. At fifty-eight he seemed far more youthful than the man who had lectured years ago in smoke-fogged halls. Contact with

206

primitive Indians and the outdoors had revived his natural optimism.

With Hentz, Catlin had tramped a hundred and fifty miles from Caracas toward Angostura on the Orinoco River. It was the season when the cattle-raising plains, or *llanos,* blossomed with flowers and darting humming-birds. Once again there was camping out, hunting, fishing—and hiking until the muscles ached. Younger men might have complained; Catlin was as happy as one of the hummingbirds.

Blocked by white men's war from Angostura, they hit the Orinoco at a lower point, and descended by canoe and steamer down the great river which Humboldt had explored. Catlin tested his old talent for charming Indians. It still worked, even with strange, stunted tribes. He painted as he traveled, and helped Dr. Hentz gather rare plants and skins of birds and animals.

Catlin eyed the husky young traveler. "We need another man for our trek up the Essequibo River to the Crystal Mountains in northern Brazil," he said. "Maybe we'll find gold!"

"I've a fine Minié rifle," Smythe said eagerly. "Just pay my expenses and supply me with powder and ball, and I'm your man."

The deal was made. Apparently Catlin had made a few timely sales for a sum adequate to finance his escape from Europe. His frugal appetites and way of living off the land when possible made travel remarkably cheap. Now his purse could bear Smythe's modest expenses without undue strain.

Before the departure, Catlin painted a few Indian tribes

of the vicinity. Then, hearing of more Indians at Pari-marbo over in Dutch Guiana, he hurried there to catch them with his brush. But at last he was ready for the trip. With a family of homeward-bound Indians and an interpreter added to their party, they pushed out into the Essequibo in a large canoe and headed upstream.

Dense tropical forests bordered the river. Birds and monkeys screamed and cackled harshly. Insects by the billion buzzed, crawled, bit. Smythe sweated, scratched, and cursed. As they paddled up the river, day after day, he could not understand how Catlin remained so cheerful.

At daybreak one morning they left the canoe to head inland. Each man carried a full load on his back. All day the guide led them through bogs and swamps. Young Smythe wearied of squishing and slipping in the muck. Catlin, with his long prairie stride, seemed tireless.

By nightfall they reached a small Indian village. Smythe wearily sank to the ground, and watched how Catlin overcame the suspicions of Indians.

The elderly chief seemed suspicious indeed. He sat with downcast head, puffing his pipe and occasionally grunting as the interpreter tried to explain the object of their mission. Finally the interpreter shrugged, and turned despairingly to Catlin.

To Smythe's surprise, Catlin suddenly began to gesture at the chief. Equally startled, the chief set aside his pipe, and watched intently the artist's expressive hands. Drawing on the sign language of the Plains Indians, and freely inventing his own pantomime, Catlin indicated his travels, his image-making, and his goodwill for Indians. Some-thing of his meaning got through to the old chief, who clapped his hands sharply, and made signs in reply. The two men smiled at each other. The first, all-important contact had been made.

Next morning Catlin continued his introduction. With variations it was a procedure he must follow with all the many tribes he visited.

"I want to show you, the great chief, and your fine people to the world," he said. The old chief looked mystified. "Just as I now show you the redskins of North America, where I come from."

Catlin opened his portfolio of bright watercolors of buffalo hunts and prairie Indians. The astonished chief examined the pictures with great excitement, then broke out into a queer, howling song which drew the entire tribe to his hut. For the rest of that day the Indians crowded about the pictures. They also exclaimed at Catlin's new six-shot carbine, which he had nicknamed "Sam."

These Indians used bows and arrows, lances, and the bola, a three-thonged rawhide weapon weighted with stones or lead. Their few guns were useless antiques. On Catlin's instructions, Smythe told the Indians, "His gun will shoot all day without stopping!"

"We do not believe," some skeptics said. "Let us see."

Smythe took an old cowhide which had been stretched on a hoop to serve as the door of a hut, painted a bull's eye in the center, and set up the target about eighty yards from Catlin.

Catlin aimed, squeezed off six shots in rapid order, and called for inspection of the target. All six shots had struck so closely together that a man's hand could cover them and the bull's eye, too. The awe-struck Indians covered their mouths with their hands. Smythe himself was startled.

"Maybe the tall tales the old boy spun back in London weren't so tall after all," he murmured to Dr. Hentz.

One of the youngsters timidly asked Catlin if he had a young rifle. Catlin smiled, and drew out his pistol. The women gasped. "Ya-ya!" they groaned. "Ya-ya, ya-ya!"

"It's very young," said Catlin, aiming at a tree about thirty yards away, "but at a short distance it's pretty good."

He fired several shots. Again the Indians clapped their hands to their mouths. Satisfied with his impression, Catlin replaced the pistol in its holster. The women shouted approvingly. "Yes, yes! Keep the poor little thing warm."

The triumph in this primitive village smoothed the way for further travel. The chief provided horses, and sent his son and nephew to guide and introduce the party to other tribes. Smythe began to understand how Catlin, with only his wits and good will to protect him, had traveled so fruitfully through thousands of miles of savage land.

Wilting under the rugged pace now set by Catlin, Dr. Hentz dropped out of the party. Catlin and Smythe pushed on through the Crystal Mountains, collecting pictures and mineral specimens.

One remote lake, with a beach pebbled by a rainbow of stones, held a special lure for Catlin. Small boys trailed him there each morning. Wide-eyed, they watched Catlin break stones with a little hammer, and then wet them with his tongue to bring out the colors. When he found a good sample he would put it in his pocket.

The boys reported to their parents that the oddest man in the world was in their midst. Every morning he ate stones for breakfast, and saved other stones for his dinner! This tribe named Catlin "Stone Eater."

"It's the Indians that draw me on," Catlin confided to Smythe. "Not the childish lure of gold. Of course, if I *should* find it, how marvelous! I'd return to the United States, get back my collection, and put it where it belongs." For a moment he saddened, recalling his tragedies.

Reluctant to speak of matters closest to his heart, he rarely mentioned his daughters. The humiliating memory of how they had last seen him as a broken and bankrupt failure still haunted him. In their letters Elizabeth, Clara, and Victoria assured him of their constant love—but wouldn't it be splendid to return to them in riches and triumph! His eyes brightened.

"Meanwhile, I'd better paint a new collection, though these poor underfed jungle lads don't move me much. If only you could see the Blackfeet, Smythe! Or a Crow warrior, with his black hair streaming behind him on his prancing horse—the proudest, freest men on earth!"

A large Indian dugout loaded with hides gave them passage down the Rio Tromboto into the vast Amazon Valley. Instead of the tall, well-shaped tribes Catlin sought, he found men stunted from meager diets, sickened by tropical diseases, sluggish from the perpetual wet heat.

"Nature bedevils them," Catlin mused, "but not as much as man. When Cabral discovered Brazil in 1500 there were three million Indians, they say, and twenty-five hundred tribes. Since then the accursed mameluko raiders have killed two million. Entire tribes have been wiped out, or led away in chains to be slaves on sugar and rubber plantations!"

The artist jumped up. Smythe had never seen him so agitated. "It's criminal!" cried Catlin. "My own country has been sinful enough in its treatment of Indians, but here—"

He paused, too overwhelmed to continue. Later, in the hostile jungles of the Amazon basins, he saw many of his noble savages who were not so noble-looking: squat bodies, feathers sprouting from holes in their cheeks, wood plugging their split lips. They warred on each other ceaselessly and senselessly. But for all that, he treated them with kindness and respect.

The party paddled hundreds of miles toward Para on the Atlantic coast. One night Catlin watched an eerie turtle hunt, under torches that cast flickering light along the banks and dark river waters.

"Good hunt," he observed, and slapped at some giant mosquitoes. "But you ought to see Comanches going after buffalo, riding like centaurs!"

Catlin painted his Indians as he found them, dwarfed by the fantastic green shapes of the jungle. In the constant, dripping humidity, he was grateful for his decision to use Bristol board, a heavy art-cardboard, instead of canvas. Canvas took too long to dry. It absorbed moisture from wet air, and buckled, peeling off paint. The thin, durable boards withstood dampness and mould, and made a fine surface for his thinly applied oils.

One afternoon they landed on a bank of the Tromboto

to roast a pig for lunch. The guide stretched out for a nap while Catlin and Smythe chatted by the fire. Suddenly Smythe noticed that Catlin was staring intently over his shoulder toward the guide.

Catlin's face was tense, but he spoke calmly. "Smythe. Keep cool, boy. Don't move an inch. There's a beautiful jaguar just behind you!"

Smythe took a deep breath, froze, and then with painfully slow caution turned his head. A large jaguar crouched beside the snoring guide. Playfully, it touched one of the guide's feet with a big paw.

Catlin slid backward down the grassy bank toward the boat. In a moment he had his rifle in hand. Grimly, he waited for the jaguar to raise its head high enough for a clear shot. At best he would have to aim dangerously close to the guide.

Catlin gave a sharp whistle. The jaguar rose higher to look at Catlin. The rifle cracked. The jaguar screeched horribly, leaped high with its claws wildly raking the air, and fell dead. The startled guide leaped even higher than the jaguar.

"Good work, Sam." Catlin patted his rifle, winked at the white-faced Smythe and calmly sat down to await his roast pig.

By the time they reached Para, on the mouth of the Amazon, Smythe was bone-weary and ready to quit.

"A bit of it's fun," he said, scratching at his varied collections of welts and jungle sores. "But I say, aren't you fed up by now with the sweat and toil, the blasted hard work and danger? How can you enjoy coping with murderous savages, after you've lived like a gentleman in London?"

Bitterness tinged Catlin's smile. "I thrive on minor problems such as headhunters. It's the jungles of Piccadilly and the Rue St. Honoré that are too dangerous for me!"

Soon the artist boarded the steamer *Marajo*, bound up the Amazon to visit Catholic missions as a means of painting Indians along the river. Smythe waved what he thought was a last farewell.

Within a month Catlin turned up again in Para. He pounced joyfully on the young Englishman, who felt rested now, and at loose ends once again.

"Smythe! The very man I need! What a dismal time I've had on the Amazon. The Catholic missions treated me well, but their Indians are overcivilized. Besides, I know little Spanish, less Portuguese, and no Amazon Indian dialects. Worst of all, this tin ear makes it devilish hard to understand translators—most of them speak broken English. Without an aide to help out, my boy, I'm absolutely lost—and here you are! Ready and waiting!"

"But—" began Smythe, and then he smiled and shrugged. He could not resist the painter's enthusiasm.

Up the Amazon they steamed, and began their descent in a small trading boat that stopped at many riverside Indian villages. These tribes were so timid and suspicious that Catlin was forced to devise ways of making his sketches without their knowledge.

With the boat anchored a few feet from shore, Catlin waited, pencil in hand, his sketchbooks and cartoon boards screened from the view of the crowds that flocked to see

214

the trading boat. It was Smythe's job to distract the Indians' attention while Catlin sketched them.

The Englishman's blazing scarlet jacket always caught their eye. They watched in awe as Smythe fired shot after shot from Catlin's repeating rifle, the first seen on the river. If this began to pall, the boatman took out his fiddle and struck up a lively tune. This often set the amused Indians to dancing. Meanwhile, Catlin made his pencil fly.

In a journey down the Amazon of a thousand miles and sixty-nine days, Catlin painted thirty different tribes.

"It's been splendid!" he said to Smythe at the end of the trip. His eyes sparkled at thought of the jaguar hunts and the time he had come to the rescue when Smythe had been treed by hundreds of peccaries eager to tear him to bits with their tusks.

This time, though, Smythe was absolutely through. He bade an amiable but weary farewell.

Having worn out the botanist and the Englishman, Catlin sought a more durable aide. He found him in Caesar Bola, a tall and powerful maroon (an escaped slave) from Havana. Quick to smile, slow to anger, oak-sturdy with his enormous chest and tree-trunk arms, Caesar looked indestructible.

They traveled thousands of miles on the Xingu, Yucayali, and Amazon rivers, for the only roads of the untamed Amazon basin were its waterways. When they neared Indian villages, Caesar often leaned forward on his rifle, offering his broad back as a handy, solid easel. Catlin rested his Bristol board against the back, and quickly sketched.

"Did you know that mural painters call their sketches

on paper cartoons, Caesar?" said Catlin. "Well, they do. And I intend to call my paintings on cardboard cartoons too. Then they won't be confused with my first collection on canvas. This, sir, will be my cartoon collection!"

"Si, señor," said Caesar. "Cartoon collection is very good. But you say we hunt for gold, señor, and all we hunt is more Indians. When we hunt for gold?"

Catlin sighed, and agreed he must be practical. Recording the primitive tribes of South America was an exciting project, but would probably earn him even less than his first collection had.

Outfitted for prospecting with a gold pan, sledge, and a chisel to cut up any gold nuggets too large to carry, they paddled up a tributary of the Amazon, and then abandoned their pirogue to cross the jungle to the mountains.

Bent under the weight of their possessions, they fought their way through an unyielding wall of perpetual dark and dank greenery.

"In the fresh air and sunshine at the tops of the trees, which we can never see," Catlin wrote wistfully, "there is a busy and chattering neighborhood of parrots and monkeys, but all below is a dark and silent matted solitude, in which a falling leaf, from want of wind, may be a month in reaching the ground, and where a man may be tracked by the broken cobwebs he leaves behind him.

"On, on we go, from day to day, cutting our way, encamping at night between our fires, serenaded by the frightful *ariguatoes* (howling monkeys), whilst we are beating off the mosquitoes, or shaving our legs to the knees with our knives to destroy the thousands of red ticks that fasten their heads in the skin. Our progress is slow. If man, like a serpent, could crawl upon his belly, he might travel faster."

But at last they broke through to rising grounds, then to open plains that showed the Crystal Mountains blue in the distance. It was easy to obtain supplies and guidance from Indians in return for knitting needles. Properly sharpened, the needles made ideal darts for blowguns.

In the mountains, thrilled by the nearness of gold that would make them rich, they followed a likely stream to an unlikely conclusion. First their mule put its hoof through the bottom of the gold pan. Then, eager to crack open some promising quartz, Caesar flexed his Herculean muscles and swung the sledge too mightily. The head flew from the shaft and plunged into deep water.

For a few minutes the angry prospectors cursed their luck. Then Catlin shrugged. "I'm just not made to accumulate gold," he said. Laughing, he picked up his brush. "Here's my talent, my only gold. Let's concentrate on that."

The two wanderers returned to the Amazon and ascended the Yucayali to the land of the Conibos, on the great prairie-like Pampa del Sacramento. Expert horsemen and hunters, the Conibos reminded Catlin of the Sioux, even though they ate turtle butter instead of buffalo marrow, and hunted with ten-foot blowguns.

"What strange poison do they put on their darts?" Catlin wondered. The Conibos shot darts at the rate of twenty a minute. One prick of poison killed a pig or a man within six minutes.

"The Conibos are very touchy these days," Catlin

217

told Caesar. "Seems European spies are trying to get their secret poison—so they can poison bullets for 'civilized' warfare!"

Irked by such prying, the Conibos fell easy prey to the threats of their jealous medicine man. With his face painted black, the medicine man chanted his death song and shook rattles at the paintings Catlin had made of Conibos.

"Here is something wonderful—and evil," he warned. "There you are with your eyes open all night. You will never sleep!"

Catlin had eased the same fear in many other tribes. This hostility, however, was too strong to master with a deft quip or a bit of flattery.

"This is a sly way to get your skins," threatened the medicine man. "Your skin will have glass eyes, and be placed with the skins of birds and snakes that white men keep!"

Some Conibos grunted in fear, and clutched their naked skins. Other picked up blowguns and sullenly eyed Catlin and Caesar. It was a time for retreat.

"I have painted you," Catlin said, "and I can unpaint you."

Quickly he brushed a coat of clay over the portraits. Later, when he and Caesar moved safely into the foot-hills of the Andes, Catlin easily washed the clay off the unharmed portraits.

As they toiled through lofty passes, Catlin marveled at the stonework left by the Incas, and mourned their defeat by the Spanish.

"I'd loved to have painted them," he said. They were

camped on a slope thousands of feet above the clouds. Giant condors with ten-foot wingspreads glided in the cold thin air, eying the big dark man and the earnest little white man who talked with such animation. "Picture them in all their glory—a mighty empire! And then think of all the poor fellows I've painted so far—Orejones and Omagues, Cocomas and Chetibos, Muras, Maranhas and Mayoroones, Ticunas, Sepibos, Yahuas, and all the rest." Catlin sighed. "Sad and hungry wretches compared to my Sioux or Crows."

Nostalgia made Catlin restless for the north, and Caesar was willing. The adventurers strode into the beautiful city of Lima, Peru, where Catlin booked passage for them both on the schooner *Sally Anne,* bound for San Francisco.

In San Francisco Catlin and some gold-hunting wanderers hired the *Sally Anne* to sail clear up the west coast to the Aleutians and Siberia's Kamchatka.

They put to port frequently. At Nootka Sound on Vancouver Island, in the dim cathedral light of British Columbia's great forest, he painted Klah-o-quats scooping out cedar logs to make long sea-going canoes. With their sharp mussel shells and chisels of elkhorn, they could build lodges a hundred feet long. They seemed a simple, orderly people—until they found a stranded whale and tore it apart in a frenzy.

When the sea was smooth on the long voyage north, Catlin worked on his sketches. In rough weather, although his increasing deafness called for many a shout, he traded tales with the others.

219

The *Sally Anne* dropped anchor long enough at Liska, in the Russian-owned Aleutian Islands, for the artist to add Aleut Indians to his collection. A few days later he set foot on Asia for the first time.

He and Caesar plodded the muddy streets of Petropavlovski, Siberia, past Russian houses of pine poles and mud toward the earth-covered mound dwellings of the Koriak Indians. Much like the Mandan mounds, thought Catlin nostalgically, although here the entrance was at the top, so that one entered by descending a ladder.

The days of this Siberian summer seemed weirdly long to Caesar. "We're getting mucho far, señor," he said wistfully, as Catlin briskly painted some Koriaks.

"True. But my legs are cramped from shipboard. Are you game for a good hike, Caesar?"

The six-foot-two maroon hesitated when Catlin pointed at a mountain blued by distance. A vast, leaning column of smoke rose from Che-nish-ka Wabe, the Mountain on Fire, the volcano of Avatcha.

"It may burn us, señor."

"Or freeze us," teased Catlin. "There's snow near the top."

"It may blow us up!"

"Let's see," said Catlin. Caesar shrugged his massive shoulders, and grinned. It might be crazy, but he was used to craziness by now.

Almost sixty now, Catlin spryly led the way up muddy lower slopes, over defiant boulders, up and up into fields of snow. They paused to don extra sweaters, then climbed upward.

Near the top, sulphur glazed the rocky cone with a

slippery coating. They peered into the crater, and saw nothing but smoke in its hissing and steaming depths. Now and then it coughed up blazing spouts of stone and gravel that whizzed past their heads.

Caesar ducked back, coughing from the choking sulphur fumes. *"Por qué?"* he muttered as he wiped his streaming eyes. Catlin was busily jotting down notes. "Why?"

Catlin explained. The painting of primitive Indians was his primary goal, by a wide margin, but another interest also concerned him.

Humboldt's books had mentioned subterranean passages into which large areas occasionally collapsed. Starting from that point Catlin had built up a theory: erosion by great underground rivers had caused collapses of enormous size, large enough to swallow fabled Atlantis, or vast prehistoric Indian civilizations.

Hunting facts to prove this theory, Catlin had begun to take notes in the Peruvian Andes. He had continued his study northward, all the way to the smoking volcanoes of Siberia. The size of caves, the appearance of fossils, dimensions of strata, the course of streams, varying tribal legends of the Great Flood—all these facts went into his notebook.

"You are a very busy man," said Caesar. His teeth flashed. "But you always have time to fish and hunt!"

"What will it be next?" said Catlin, his face lighting up. "A crack at seals? Or maybe a polar bear?"

On the return voyage the coastal Nayas caught Catlin's eye. Their cedar canoes were as sleek and gay as

Venetian gondolas. The women wore bright-hued mantles of wool and dog hair. The men smoked long, elaborately carved pipes of jet-black stone.

Naturally the discoverer of catlinite, the red pipestone, was interested. He studied the writhing interlocked figures of men and animals carved in the stone. Caesar found more amusement in the masquerade dance. Behind their droll masks and costumes, the medicine men proclaimed themselves "King of Loons," "Doctor of the Rabbits," "King of the Bustards," and similar titles. Caesar's lusty laughter almost broke up the dance.

Catlin painted other British Columbia tribes, such as the Hydas, Bella Bellas, Skidegates and Stickeens. Ready by then for dinner in a civilized restaurant with tablecloths, Catlin and Caesar left the schooner, when it grounded in the Strait of Juan de Fuca, and hiked into Victoria.

Catlin gazed at the town aghast. The madness of the Fraser River gold rush had gripped the town. Every house, steamer and shack bulged with occupants. Men and women slept in carts and wagons on the streets. Others caroused away the night, dancing and drinking around bonfires.

Catlin was immune to gold fever now. "Let's get out of this madhouse," he said.

They sailed for Astoria, at the mouth of the Columbia River, and ascended that broad river to The Dalles. The many Indians assembled at this famous salmon-catching narrows were quickly added to his collection: Walla Wallas, Klatsops, Chinooks, Nez Perces, Clikatats, Spokane.

A rumor that a party of Crows was encamped in the Salmon River Valley stirred happy memories.

"Crows!" exclaimed Catlin to Caesar, who by now had seen enough Indians to last him several lifetimes. "You must see them!"

Although warned that the valley was remote, and far too difficult a journey for a man his age, Catlin promptly bought a horse and a couple of mules, and set out.

The long ride developed into a long hike, for most of the time the men had to lead their animals up steep trails. They trudged up the Columbia, up the Snake River, and on into the Rockies.

While they cooled their blistered feet in an icy mountain stream near the end of a grueling day, Catlin looked thoughtfully at the jumble of enormous blocks of gneiss and granite on the mountainsides. Soon he wandered off with his notebook.

"A stupendous mountain," he wrote, "with its hidden treasures from the bottom of the sea, has been lifted up to the heavens and, crumbling to pieces, is tumbling into the valley and ravines below! What a field for the geologist to get at the deepest productions of the earth's hidden material—and why are the geologists not here?"

He scribbled on and on, then set aside his notebook to ponder the mysterious and mighty movements of the earth.

It was dark when he returned to camp, and his stumbling awoke Caesar and the mules. Caesar rose on one elbow and stared sleepily at him.

"Señor Catlin," he said, "you a very strange hombre, that's all I got to say!"

On the eighth day a beautiful valley opened out beneath them. On the tenth day Catlin stiffened at sight of a far-off spire of smoke. He squinted into the distance, then chuckled.

"See those skin tepees? That's a Crow village!"

As a sort of passport and credential, Catlin always carried samples of his paintings with him. In the Crow camp the tall long-haired warriors gathered to look at the portraits. Suddenly one of them shouted, "Bi-eets-ee-cure! Bi-eets-ee-cure!"

Bi-eets-ee-cure, The Very Sweet Man, painted twenty-two years before by Catlin, was only a short distance away at the fish-drying banks. The old portrait had immediately been recognized. The Very Sweet Man was summoned, and he and Catlin launched into long and lively reminiscence of the good old days at Fort Union.

On the return, Catlin and Caesar joined the haggard survivors of an Oregon-bound wagon train, and helped them descend the Snake River. From Portland they sailed down the coast to San Diego, in southern California.

There Caesar sighed deeply at the sight of new mules and Catlin poring over maps.

"More Indians?" asked Caesar.

"More Indians."

Caesar sighed again, even more deeply. Although his muscles rippled as mightily as ever, he was wearying. Nevertheless, he rode inland with Catlin to the Ghiba Apache village.

Catlin painted a contest in which mounted Apache warriors thundered over a field at full gallop to shoot ten arrows into ten circular targets on the ground. He also carefully recorded a craft rarely seen by whites, the manufacture of flint arrowheads. A master workman cradled a flake of flint in the palm of one hand, and pressed a chisel to it. To the chanting of a special song, his helper struck the chisel with a mallet, chipping away the flint exactly in time with the music.

After crossing the Rockies via the Santa Fe pass, the wanderers turned southward to the Rio Grande to avoid a war between Apaches and United States troops. Once again they took to paddles. Eight hundred miles downstream at Matamoros on the Gulf of Mexico, they boarded ship for Sisal, in Yucatan.

There they parted. Although Sally Bool, the beautiful mulatto girl who sold oranges on the quay in Para, was still waiting to hear of the wonders of Caesar's travels, he feared she might not wait much longer.

Deeply moved by their farewells after many thousands of miles of wandering together on three continents, they shook hands three times. With each shake Caesar said fervently, "May the Lord preserve you. May the Lord preserve you."

And so even the giant Caesar Bola had at last cried enough—but Catlin wandered on.

Hundreds of years ago the Mayans of Yucatan had invented calendars, made precise astronomical observations, and reared great stone temples that rivaled the pyramids of Egypt. Now their dead cities were drowned in a sea of green jungle.

As Catlin hacked away greenery at Uxmal to observe grotesque stone statues, he became convinced more than ever that in accordance with his geological theories some marvelous Indian Atlantis had suddenly disappeared even more completely than the Mayans, under a sea of water.

To pursue his theory of collapses in the earth's crust he needed the help of a trained scientist. What better man could there be than Baron Alexander von Humboldt? This good friend had provided the seed for Catlin's idea.

If Humboldt accepted the theory and published it, the scientific world would hail Catlin for solving a great mystery. Then Dudley Gregory would stop looking down his nose at his failure brother-in-law. Instead of apologizing for their father, the Catlin girls would be proud of him once more.

Bubbling with high hopes, Catlin sailed in the late spring of 1855 for Europe and Baron von Humboldt.

Ojibway Pipe

Peh-to-pee-kiss, The Eagle Ribs, Blackfoot War Chief,
Wife and Child

17: Last Rambles

THE OLD man paced like a youth in his overheated study
in Berlin. From time to time he shot a penetrating question in English or German. His brow was as smooth as
a baby's, his eyes as bright as a child's, but this was the
aged Baron von Humboldt, one of the great men of the
nineteenth century.

Napoleon, Beethoven, Jefferson, and Goethe had paid
him homage. Now the famous scientist and explorer,
though hard at work on the massive volumes of his
Kosmos, listened with excitement to the theories of the
sinewy brown American artist.

Catlin presented many facts to back his theory of hot
underground rivers eroding the earth's crust. He believed
that the floor of the Caribbean Sea and the Gulf of

227

Mexico had once been a broad and fertile plain dotted with monumental cities rivaling ancient Rome and Babylon. The sudden collapse of eroded caverns had toppled these cities in horrible scenes of disaster, to become drowned kingdoms under the sea.

Two seething underground rivers, Catlin added, flowed under the Rockies and the Andes in torrents that would make the Amazon seem like a tiny stream. Welling out together under the Atlantic, they provided the warmth and current of the Gulf Stream.

The scope of the idea appealed to Humboldt. He seized Catlin's hand and congratulated him. "This could be very important," he said. "But there is much work to be done. We'll have a lot to talk about, Herr Catlin, after I study your notes."

Through Humboldt's generous assistance, Catlin met the King and Queen of Prussia, who bought some of his paintings. This sale and others, plus accumulated royalties, gave Catlin enough funds for the return expedition which Humboldt said was necessary.

"Facts! We must have facts, and still more facts," said the baron. "I'll draw up a list of the places to visit, and of the evidence you must seek."

It was a cheery, optimistic Catlin who sailed in September, 1855, for the West Indies. He cherished Humboldt's farewell note. If only he were younger, wrote the scientist, he would join the expedition. The discoveries might cast important light on how cataclysms affected the distribution of the races.

Nothing must stop Catlin, he said, on his noble mission.

As always, Catlin took his painting materials and Bristol boards on his rambles. No new Indian tribe would ever escape *him!* But he also carried detailed instructions from Humboldt.

Puzzled natives on the shores of Antigua, Trinidad, St. Thomas, Tortugas, Granada, and Jamaica saw the lean lively man sampling the waters and the sands. He explored the islands; he inspected ocean currents; he studied mountain ranges. In Venezuela he made notes on the Caracas escarpment, the Gulf of Maracaibo, the capes of Santa Martha.

Ranging far south to Buenos Aires, Argentina, Catlin joined forces with a half-breed guide, José Alzar, to paddle far up the Paraguay River. They crossed by land from Candeloria to the Uraguay River, which they started to descend in a large pirogue.

It was a splendid trip, mused Catlin as he scanned the river bank for signs of the jaguars that preyed on peccaries and turtles along the shores. Interesting minerals and interesting Indians—like the naked Payaguas, taller even than Osages, who all dwelt in one *tolderia,* a long open shed.

And the hunting! What if the dim hearing left in one ear *did* make jungle hunting a bit risky? His eye was keen, his hand steady—and his mouth watering at thought of jaguar tail. Take a fat tail, say six or eight pounds, wrap it in wild cabbage leaves, properly roast it under the embers of a campfire, and taste! Ah, what a delicacy! Besides, one must be practical, and remember that a jaguar skin sold for twenty dollars.

"To go down stream in a solid and dry canoe, in such

a climate, on so clear and beautiful a river, with hard biscuits enough, and coffee and sugar and salt, and a few pounds of salt pork for cooking, and plenty of powder and ball and fishing tackle," wrote Catlin contentedly, "is one of the delightful things in the world."

In this paradise where fish, ducks and geese abounded, and the river islands were fragrant with luscious oranges and wild peaches, what was the great hazard? Jaguars, rattlesnakes, hostile Indians? No. He slapped at a villain whining about his ear. The mosquito! He had fought this puny pest in river valleys from the Missouri to the Amazon. Immense clouds of relentless torturers declared war at every sundown. Often Catlin's party fled from the camp to midstream, hiding in the canoe for hours until the savagery abated.

"One must be practical," said Catlin, with a twinkle in his eye, and handed Alzar his recipe for Mosquito Soup. It suggested a method of trapping hordes of mosquitoes in a kettle of boiling water. Season with salt pork, pepper and tiny wild onions, and the result would be a nutritious soup.

Alzar never had a chance to test the recipe. He stiffened and pointed at the sandy shore. The great numbers of turtle shells and half-eaten turtles were a sure sign of jaguars.

Catlin immediately seized Sam, his Colt carbine. A moment later he spotted the head of a large jaguar craning above the grass atop the high bank. He nudged Alzar, who silently glided the craft closer to shore. The veteran hunter sighted carefully, squeezed the trigger. With the crack of his rifle the jaguar disappeared.

230

"Dead shot, señor!" cried the men.

"Perhaps," said Catlin. The pirogue grated against the sand, and Catlin sprang out and peered up at the point where the jaguar had been. The steep weedy bank rose more than thirty feet. Hidden at its brink might be the wounded jaguar, waiting—or an enraged mate might be at its side.

Still, there were five shots left in Sam. Catlin gestured for Alzar to remain in the pirogue with his own rifle ready, and he scrambled up the bank.

As he neared the top, his pace slowed. He held his rifle raised above him. Behind the dense green curtain of reeds was—what? He cocked his head, straining to hear the sound of an animal breathing, a paw treading, or a tail lashing against the reeds. His faded hearing detected nothing.

Cautiously, his heart fluttering like a trapped bird, he eased himself over the crest.

As if shot from a cannon the snarling jaguar struck. The impact cartwheeled Catlin down the cliff. His senseless and bleeding body lay motionless at the river's edge. Poised above for the kill, the jaguar lashed his tail and growled. A timely volley of shots from José and the boatman rang out, and the lithe beast bounded away.

While Catlin recuperated in Buenos Aires, he learned another serious attack had been made upon him. Schoolcraft's official six-volume work on Indians was being published. On June 9, 1856, Humboldt fired off an indignant letter from Potsdam, hoping it would reach Catlin in Uruguay.

"An immense scrapbook on the North American Indians, written by Schoolcraft, has been sent me. He denies the truth of the Mandan Religious Ceremonies, saying that they are contrary to facts, and the works of your imagination. Now, my dear and esteemed friend, this charge, made by such a man as Schoolcraft and *under the authority of the Government of the United States,* to stand in the libraries of the scientific institutions of the whole world, to which they are being sent as presents from your Government, is calculated not only to injure your hard-earned good name, but to destroy the value of your precious works, through all ages, unless you take immediate steps to counteract its effects."

The infuriating news set Catlin musing on ways to combat the injustice once he had completed his expedition.

Meanwhile, a pleasant interlude speeded his recovery. Alzar had introduced him to a charming young brother and sister visiting from their Auca tribe on the Rio Salado. Til-tee, The Little Firefly, enchanted Catlin with her tawny beauty and graceful manner. As she leafed respectfully through his portfolio, she said, "Our country is prettier. The forests are bigger, the lakes more beautiful. The pampas stretch out forever. There are ostriches and wild cattle to chase, and Indian games—oh, you must come!"

It was the kind of invitation Catlin never could resist. Within a few days he was astride a silvery stallion with a flowing black mane and tail, racing over the pampas and marveling at the horsemanship of the Aucas.

"They're as good as Comanches!" he shouted to Alzar

over the beat of pounding hoofs. "Incredible!"

They flung whirling bolas to down their fleeing prey, and rarely missed. With Til-tee watching, Catlin took after an ostrich to show his own prowess. His blood tingled as he pursued the big bird, which zigzagged at astonishing speed. With one shot fired at full gallop he brought it down. Til-tee, racing along after him, uttered a cheer, and clapped her hands.

A suspicion that these might be his last great days afield made the visit even sweeter. He plodded happily through knee-deep muck in salt marshes, where thousands of flamingoes flapped up noisily from their mounded nests. He fired away, and they fell like scarlet rain.

His ostrich plumes and flamingo feathers would be tributes to Til-tee. He thought of her through a solitary night spent in the flamingo marshes. Glowing clouds of fireflies hovered and danced, appeared and disappeared, as luminous and as fitful as the love for him that seemed to glow in Til-tee's eyes. If he chose he could spend his last years in this Eden, warmed by her devotion. Why go on suffering and fighting for his collection and his cause, in a world that had rejected both?

But at sixty Catlin knew he could never abandon his life work, no matter how hopeless or unrewarding it might seem. He still had research before him—and another collection to complete!

He left lovely Til-tee late in 1856, sailed to Tierra del Fuego at the foot of the continent, and up the west coast to Panama. After crossing the isthmus in 1857 he inspected the lakes and mountains of Venezuela.

Although mail service was nonexistent in many of

233

the wild areas he visited, he had kept in touch with his daughters and his brother Francis. Occasionally letters, many months old, had straggled out of the jungle. Furthermore, an old friend of his Albany days, Professor Henry, now head of the Smithsonian Institution, had sent letters to all U. S. consuls in South America asking them to forward any news of Catlin. Now this source dried up.

When no letters came for a full year, Francis appealed to the State Department for help, but in vain. If Catlin sent letters, they must have sunk to the bottom of some tropic stream. For almost two years Catlin holed up, apparently in some remote village, and worked furiously to complete research, paintings, and manuscripts of new books.

At last he sailed for Europe for the proud presentation of his work to Humboldt—and then he heard the crushing news. Baron von Humboldt had died!

As he paced the deck and stared at the gray sea, Catlin faced up to the bitter truth: without Humboldt's prestige behind it, his theory would be ignored. All his years of arduous travel and painstaking research had been wasted.

It was enough to make a strong man weep. Catlin reacted by going to his cabin for one of his unfinished paintings. He spread out his colors, and started to work. Misfortunes came and went; Indians and painting endured.

Sauk. Keokuk, His Wife and a Warrior

18: The Last Battle

"PLEASE, MR. CATLIN," shouted the publisher. "Haven't you another book for us?"

George Catlin smiled, and shook his head. Fearing the deaf author had misunderstood, the publisher hopefully wrote out his query, but again Catlin shook his head.

It was 1862. At the age of sixty-six Catlin was once again riding high in London, thanks to publication of the works he had written in South America.

"Surely you don't want another *Steam Raft?*" said Catlin slyly, referring to a pamphlet published just before his return to England. Sub-titled *Suggested as a Means of Security to Human Life upon the Ocean,* it advanced the idea of huge unsinkable rafts made of layers of hollow cottonwood logs, propelled by bucket-and-chain drives.

"No, no," said the publisher hastily. "A book! Something like *Life Amongst the Indians!*"

This book had been aimed at boys. Packed with Indian lore and thrilling accounts of Catlin's adventures with Indians, rattlers, grizzlies and jaguars in the wilderness of two continents, it became an immediate best seller. Indeed, it sold well for many years thereafter.

"Or maybe another health book!" shouted the publisher. "Your public is waiting!"

In 1861 Catlin's odd little health book had been published. Usually entitled *Mal-respiration and its effects upon the enjoyments and life of Man,* its later title conveys the basic idea more pithily—*Shut Your Mouth and Save Your Life.*

Sleep on your back, breathe through the nose, and keep your mouth shut tight, said Catlin. By so doing the Indians prevented snoring, nightmares, insomnia, fits, decayed teeth, deformity, colds and contagions.

Illustrated with fantastic and comical drawings to show the dangers of improper breathing, the book sold more than forty thousand copies.

"The public will have to wait a few years, I'm afraid," said Catlin. "Tomorrow I leave for Brussels, and there I plan to stay."

His London friends were bewildered by the move. Catlin knew few people in Brussels; in the years he spent there he saw little of the city.

"Maybe it's his deafness," theorized a friend. "He used to be so social—and now conversing is so difficult he's becoming something of a hermit."

What Catlin wanted above all, however, was to conserve his waning energies for one last great effort. He wanted no distractions from his battle to salvage his Indian collection and to restore his reputation as an Indian expert.

A bad book and gaudy showmanship had harmed him in London. In America there had been smears from Indian haters and exploiters, fur traders, slaveholders, and jealous competitors such as Schoolcraft. A cloud lingered about his name and he meant to dispel it.

General A. L. Chetlain of Chicago, the American consul at Brussels, walked down an obscure street near the Antwerp railroad station to call on his eccentric friend.

"Fine chap," Chetlain had told others. "Bit of a recluse, but a charming and interesting talker once he gets going."

Chetlain climbed to the second floor, and entered the large front room. It was scantily furnished, and used as an exhibition room and studio. Hanging on the walls were cartoons, as Catlin termed all his later paintings on Bristol board.

Except for some lovely jungle landscapes and hunting scenes these thinly painted oils could not compare artistically with Catlin's first collection. At Humboldt's suggestion he had usually depicted full-length groups of Indians on each panel. Unfortunately, this showed up his weakness at drawing figures and wasted his great talent for individual portraits. The cartoons, nevertheless, made an appealing and valuable collection.

Catlin looked up from his easel, and advanced toward his friend with a quick, firm step.

"Ah, Chetlain!" he cried, in the overloud monotone of the deaf. "Good to see you. I've been thinking over our chat about the Black Hawk War, and its ironic aspects." His lined face was eager. "After the whites slaughtered Black Hawk's people—men, women and children after they repeatedly tried to surrender—they hailed Black Hawk as a hero on his tour of the east. While he was still a prisoner! A university gave him an honorary degree—"

He launched into reminiscence of Black Hawk and Keokuk. Occasionally Chetlain shouted a comment or scribbled a reply on a piece of paper. Sometimes Catlin, too, wrote his answers.

"Come for dinner tonight!" Chetlain shouted. "Dinner—tonight!"

Catlin nodded. As soon as the consul left, he was back at his easel.

Chetlain often wondered about Catlin. The artist avoided all strangers now, even his own countrymen and fellow artists. He never spoke of his family or explained his present way of life. Apart from an occasional break-fast or dinner at Chetlain's, Catlin was almost a hermit. Sometimes he ate frugally at an adjoining restaurant; more often he took his favorite meal of bread and milk at home. He slept in a small rear room which was also used for storage.

For a man of seventy he was robust and active, Chetlain mused, so why did he spend these long and lonely years in Brussels?

In those simple, quiet years Catlin worked as few young men could. He wrote letters to American museums and historical societies, imploring them to rescue his Indian Gallery from the boiler works factory where it was mouldering.

He wrote a short book, *O-kee-pa,* published in 1867. Designed to disprove Schoolcraft's charges of fraud, it was a detailed illustrated account of the Mandan religious rites. Included were testimonies to its accuracy from James Kipp and others.

He sent a copy of *O-kee-pa* to Congress with a long history of his Indian Gallery, the campaign of the past for congress to buy it, and the efforts of Schoolcraft to block the purchase.

Schoolcraft had fed in comfort and security upon the Government crib, he wrote scornfully, while Catlin had risked his life and spent his last cent to gather information in the Indian wilderness. But with the aid of a "whiskey seller"—D. D. Mitchell, Superintendent of Indian Affairs, a former fur trader who had never even been permitted to see the Mandan ceremonies—Schoolcraft had blackened his name.

Therefore, said Catlin, Congress should purchase copies of *O-kee-pa,* without profit to Catlin, and send a copy to every library to which it had given the maligning Schoolcraft volumes.

No action was taken by Congress. Catlin, in his early seventies, continued his lonely battle.

Each year he completed fifty or sixty cartoon paintings, not only of Indians seen on his later rambles; but copies as well of the paintings of his original Indian Gallery.

"If my first collection is ignored, abused, and rotting

away," he said, "I'll bring back another to the United States—just as big, and even better!"

In 1868 he published another book meant for boys, *Last Rambles Amongst the Indians of the Rocky Mountains and the Andes.* Although poorly organized, and confusing as to routes and years, it contained some lively tales of his travels.

In 1869, fearing at seventy-three that death might come before he could salvage his collection, he wrote to his brother Francis to try to sell the paintings to the New York Historical Society. His brother's efforts failed.

At last Catlin showed his cartoon collection of hundreds of oils. The display was well received in Brussels. Encouraged, Catlin now sought to bolster his reputation as a scientist with the publication of *The Lifted and Subsided Rocks of America.* Its 228 pages of evidence supporting the geological and anthropological theories which had interested Humboldt attracted little notice.

One autumn day in 1870 a steamer edged in to a New York pier. At the age of seventy-four, after an absence of thirty-one years, George Catlin was returning to New York. Still erect and alert despite his graying hair and lined face, he strode down the gangplank with an assurance that masked a tangle of emotions.

As he searched for a familiar face in the crowd waiting on the pier, his heart sank. He recognized no one. Then he looked again at a trio of well-dressed young women. Was it possible they were his daughters, the little girls he had last seen in London? He swallowed hard. Something about their stance and the set of their eyes reminded him of his long-dead Clara. And there, that middle-aged man joining them—it was his youngest brother Francis!

After the long years they stared at him uncertainly. He hurried toward them, tears glinting in his eyes.

"Elizabeth," he said, and opened his arms wide. "Clara, Victoria!"

They rushed toward him, and he closed his arms tightly about them. Their fresh young lips pressed against his withered cheeks. Although his world was silent, he knew they were crying, "Father! Father!" Francis shouted vainly, and made gestures to indicate his happiness.

At last Catlin stood back and took a good look at his weeping, smiling girls. Although he had wandered half the world while they grew up, it seemed that they miraculously had their mother's understanding. If he had been a stay-at-home father, he would not have been the George Catlin they loved and admired.

The prosperous Catlin girls hoped to make up for their father's hardships. Elizabeth scribbled an appeal, and held it for him to read: "Father, please come live with me. It's time you had some peace and comfort!"

Catlin's smile of gratitude was warm and tender. How could he make them understand that he had never sought peace and comfort—and never would.

He shook his head, and said simply, "I still have a lifetime's work to do."

As independent and full of plans as ever, he took a hotel room in Manhattan, and in October opened his cartoon exhibit at the Somerville Gallery on Fifth Avenue. "This will restore my reputation," he told Francis, as he labored over posters, newspaper advertising, and the hanging of an immense show of six hundred oils. "A whole new generation has grown up to learn about my Indians!"

A few weeks later he sadly announced the closing of his show. His cartoon collection, although not the equal of his original collection as art or science, made a valuable and exciting display. But the timing of the exhibit could not have been worse. The infamous Boss Tweed scandals broke, and the newspapers had room for nothing else. Then P. T. Barnum bellowed into town with The Greatest Show on Earth. His lavish publicity smothered poor Catlin's more modest ads.

In this hour of distress, Professor Joseph Henry, Secretary and Director of the Smithsonian, invited Catlin to hang his show there, and to stay in a little room high in one of the turrets. Catlin almost wept for joy. At last his paintings were to hang in a National Museum!

With his show hanging as a close reminder, Catlin hoped that at last Congress would act on the acquisition of his buried collection. He labored over petitions to Congress, made drawings, and touched up paintings even as they hung in the Smithsonian. Happily, he explained his cartoons to visitors.

Congressmen talked sympathetically, but did not act. As months passed, Catlin began to fear he was only a charity case, tolerated because of his old friendship with Henry. It was more than his pride could bear. His last battle, he realized, was a losing one.

At seventy-six, his gallant spirit waned. In late autumn of 1872 he fell ill. Stoic as an Indian, he fought the agony of incurable Bright's disease alone in the turret room. In spite of his pain he was kind and thoughtful to the boy who delivered his food.

"I was lucky," he had written about the Indians, "to have been born at the right time to see these people in their native dignity. With my toils and privations, I have had my enjoyments. My works are done, and as well as I could do them. Artists of future ages may look in vain for another race so picturesque . . .

"I was lucky," he repeated on his sick bed.

Inevitably he recalled his Indian credo:

"I love the people who have always made me welcome to the best they had.

". . . who are honest without laws, who have no jails and no poorhouses.

". . . who keep the commandments without ever having read them or heard them preached from the pulpit.

". . . who love their neighbors as they love themselves.

". . . who worship God without a bible, for I believe that God loves them also.

". . . whose religion is all the same, and who are free from religious animosities.

". . . who have never raised a hand against me, or stolen my property, where there was no law to punish for either.

". . . who have never fought a battle with white men, except on their own ground.

"I love and don't fear mankind where God has made and left them, for there they are children.

"I love a people who live, and keep what is their own, without locks and keys.

"I love all people who do the best they can. And, oh, how I love a people who don't live for the love of money."

When he was too weak to protest, his daughters removed him to Jersey City, and gave him every possible care. One day he rose and paced the floor until his little store of strength gave out, saying, "Oh, if I were down in the valley of the Amazon I could walk off this weakness." The fate of his Indian Gallery troubled him more than the pain of his disease.

As he lay dying a terrible anguish seized him, and he rose, crying, "What will become of my Gallery! What will become of my Gallery!"

Out on his beloved prairies a fantastic slaughter was in full swing. Long trains steamed eastward loaded with buffalo meat and hides. A stench of rotting carcasses hung over plains white from a blizzard of bones. Within eleven years the ruthless butchery would reduce the herds from five million to seven hundred and forty.

The death of the buffalo meant death for the Plains Indians. The way of life Catlin had loved was dying. It was a fitting time for him to go, too.

He died on the twenty-third of December, 1872.

244

Epilogue

FOR ALMOST ninety years Catlin lay in an unmarked grave in Greenwood Cemetery, Brooklyn, beside his wife and son. The absence of even a simple headstone symbolized the neglect and obscurity of this remarkable and once-famous man.

Slowly his star rose anew.

In 1879 the Indian Gallery was at last rescued from the boiler works and turned over to the National Museum of the Smithsonian Institution—445 paintings had survived. In 1912 the American Museum of Natural History in New York acquired 418 paintings from his cartoon collection. Thousands of his pencil drawings are in the New York Public Library, New York Historical Society, Newberry Library of Chicago, and Yale University.

Historians and ethnologists never really forgot Catlin. As a documentary painter of unrivalled industry he passed on a vast store of solid information about Indians. Because he traveled too far and too fast for careful study, his hasty painting and writing contain some notable errors. But these are mere dents and scratches in a monument of pure gold.

Even at his peak Catlin's paintings were praised for their novel subject matter, rather than as art. Only Baudelaire foreshadowed the appreciation of contemporary authorities like Perry Rathbone of the Boston Museum of Fine Arts, who admire the freshness and vigor of his work. Moderns praise the excitement and wonder that glow through Catlin's deft works, reflecting his deep feeling about his Indians and prairies.

The National Museum now receives requests by the score from other museums for loans of Catlin's works. His reputation as an artist has never been higher.

His basic cause, to preserve the appearance and customs of the Indian, was a success. Because he showed us what they looked like, Western movies and television shows, popular fiction and illustrations are all shaped somewhat by Catlin. When the world thinks of Indians it usually thinks of the Plains Indian as seen through his warm and sympathetic eye.

His crusade to depict the Indian as a noble people suffering outrageous injustice was less successful. Even this fight is at last being won, however, as prejudice and cruelty toward the original Americans steadily diminish, and we look honestly at both sides of our history.

At last, in the spring of 1961, a small band of admirers gathered in Greenwood Cemetery to pay tardy honor to a great man.

A gray granite headstone inscribed GEORGE CATLIN 1796–1872 was placed on a grassy knoll ringed with ivy. As they stood under an ancient holly tree the group heard a reading of Chapter 44 of Ecclesiasticus, beginning "Let us now praise famous men."

Selected Bibliography

BOOKS:

Bizardel, Yvon. *American Painters in Paris*. New York: Macmillan, 1960.

Carmer, Carl. *The Susquehannah*. New York: Rinehart, 1955.

Catlin, George. *Letters and Notes on the Manners, Customs, and Condition of the North American Indians*. Published by the author. London: 1841. 2 vols.

————. *Catlin's Notes of Eight Years' Travel and Residence in Europe*. Published by the author. London: 1848.

————. *Life Amongst the Indians*. London: Sampson, Low, 1861.

————. *The Breath of Life, or Mal-respiration*. New York: J. Wiley, 1861.

————. *O-Kee-pa: A Religious Ceremony*. London: Trubner & Co., 1867.

————. *Last Rambles Amongst the Indians of the Rocky Mountains and the Andes*. New York: D. Appleton & Co., 1867.

————. *George Catlin*, edited by Marvin C. Ross, Norman, Oklahoma: University of Oklahoma Press, 1959.

Chittenden, Hiram M. *The American Fur Trade of the Far West*. New York: Francis P. Harper, 1902. 2 vols.

————. *The History of Early Steamboat Navigation on*

the Missouri River. New York: Francis P. Harper, 1903.

DeVoto, Bernard. *Across the Wide Missouri*. Boston: Houghton Mifflin, 1947.

————. *The Journals of Lewis and Clark* (edited). Boston: Houghton Mifflin, 1953.

Dodge, Col. Richard. *Our Wild Indians*. Hartford, Conn.: Worthington & Co., 1883.

Donaldson, Thomas. "The George Catlin Indian Gallery." In Annual Report of Smithsonian Institution for 1885. Washington, D.C.

Ewers, John C. "George Catlin, Painter of Indians and the West." From the Smithsonian Report for 1955, Washington, D.C.

Gardiner, Dorothy. *West of the River*. New York: Crowell, 1941.

Haberly, Lloyd. *Pursuit of the Horizon*. New York: Macmillan, 1948.

McCracken, Harold. *George Catlin and the Old Frontier*. New York: Dial Press, 1959.

Quimby, George. *Indians of the Western Frontier*. Chicago: Chicago Natural History Museum, 1954.

Webb, Walter P. *The Great Plains* New York: Ginn & Co., 1931.

PERIODICALS:

American Heritage. April 1955. "The Peales" by Oliver Jensen.

Art in America. No. 1, 1961. "Rediscovery: Catlin in the Smithsonian Institution" by Perry T. Rathbone.

The Literary Collector. October 1901. "George Catlin," by William Harvey Miner.

New York Times. September 5, 1910; May 18, 1961.

248